Graham Cowley for Royal Court Theatre Productions Ltd

in association with Bill Kenwright for Bill Kenwright Ltd

presents the Royal Court Theatre production

John Sessions   **David Bamber**

Anthony Calf   **Joe Duttine**

Roger Frost   **Kenneth MacDonald**

MY NIGHT
with
RE G

by Kevin Elyot

Director Roger Michell

Designer William Dudley

Lighting Jon Linstrum

**CRITERION
THEATRE**

First performed at the Royal Court T

First performed at the Criterion

Sue TOWNSEND'S THE QUEEN AND I

DIRECTOR
ROGER MICHELL

DESIGNER
WILLIAM DUDLEY

LIGHTING DESIGNER
JON LINSTRUM

SOUND DESIGNER
PAUL ARDITTI

COMPANY STAGE MANAGER
SHEENA LINDEN

DEPUTY STAGE MANAGER
HEDDA MOORE

ASSISTANT STAGE MANAGER
ELIZABETH THOMPSON

CASTING
LISA MAKIN

ASSISTANT DIRECTOR
JEREMY HERRIN

PRODUCTION MANAGER
BO BARTON

COSTUME SUPERVISOR
GLENDA NASH

WARDROBE MISTRESS
KATE ELLIOTT

PRODUCTION ELECTRICIAN
FELIX DAVIES

PRODUCTION CARPENTER
NICK COLLIE

SET BUILT BY
SCOTT FLEARY

PRODUCTION PHOTOGRAPHY
MARK DOUET

LEAFLET AND POSTER DESIGN
THE LOFT

PHOTOGRAPHY FOR LEAFLET, POSTER
AND FRONT OF HOUSE
MATTHEW WARD

ADDITIONAL MODEL FOR LEAFLET
PIERS ALLEN

PLAYTEXT ADDITIONAL PAGES
SIGHTLINES

David Bamber

left to right including foreground
David Bamber, Joe Duttine, Kenneth MacDonald and **Roger Frost**

left to right
Kenneth MacDonald and **Roger Frost**

Anthony Calf   photos Ivan Kyncl

CAST

in order of speaking

JOHN **ANTHONY CALF**

GUY **DAVID BAMBER**

ERIC **JOE DUTTINE**

DANIEL **JOHN SESSIONS**

BERNIE **ROGER FROST**

BENNY **KENNETH MACDONALD**

There will be no interval
The performance lasts approximately 1 hour 40 minutes

John Sessions (background) and **David Bamber** (foreground)

KEVIN ELYOT
(Writer)

For the Royal Court: **My Night With Reg** (1994 Writers' Guild of Great Britain Award for Best Fringe Theatre Play).

Other theatre: **Coming Clean** (Bush / 1982 Samuel Beckett Award); **Consent** (Horseshoe Theatre Company); **The Moonstone,** adapted from the novel by Wilkie Collins (Swan,Worcester); **Artists & Admirers**, a new translation of Ostrovsky's play (RSC).

TV: **Killing Time** (BBC / 1991 Writers' Guild of Great Britain Award for Best Television Play or Film).

Currently: the television adaptation of Alan Hollinghurst's **The Swimming-Pool Library** (BBC / Freeway Films).

Radio: **According to Plan**; **The Perfect Moment** (both for the BBC); **The Double Dealer**, an adaptation of Congreve's play (to be broadcast in 1995).

Film: **Infatuation** (BBC Films); **The Silence of the Sirens** (Arenal Productores Asociados / European Script Fund); and currently, **Murder in the Heart** (BBC Films).

Kevin Elyot is also an actor.

PAUL ARDITTI
(Sound Designer)

For the Royal Court: **Babies, Some Voices, Thyestes, My Night With Reg, The Kitchen, The Madness of Esme and Shaz, Hammett's Apprentice, Hysteria, Live Like Pigs, Search and Destroy**.

Other theatre sound design includes: **Hamlet** (Peter Hall Company); **St Joan** (Strand); **The Winter's Tale, Cymbeline, The Tempest, Antony and Cleopatra, The Trackers of Oxyrhynchus** (Royal National Theatre); **The Gift of the Gorgon** (RSC & Wyndham's); **Orpheus Descending** (Haymarket & Broadway); **A Streetcar Named Desire** (Bristol Old Vic); **The Winter's Tale** (Manchester Royal Exchange); **The Wild Duck** (Phoenix); **Henry IV, The Ride Down Mount Morgan** (Wyndham's) **Born Again** (Chichester Festival); **Three Sisters, Matador** (Queen's); **Twelfth Night, The Rose Tattoo** (Playhouse); **Becket, Cyrano de Bergerac** (Haymarket); **Travesties** (Savoy); **Four Baboons Adoring The Sun** (Lincoln Centre, 1992 Drama Desk Award); **Piaf** (Piccadilly). Opera includes: **Gawain and the Green Knight (**ROH).

TV includes: **The Camomile Lawn**.

DAVID BAMBER
(Guy)

Trained at **RADA** where he was awarded the Bancroft Gold Medal.

For the Royal Court: **Byrthrite, Karate Billy Comes Home, Three Birds Alighting on a Field, Search and Destroy, My Night With Reg, Young Writers Festival** including **The Arbor**.

Other London theatre: Shostakovich in **Masterclass** (Old Vic & Wyndham's); **Heroes** and **Progress,** both Doug Lucie (New End and Bush); **Kissing God** (Hampstead); Hiketier in **Schippel the Plumber** (Greenwich 1992 and 1993). For the RNT: **Oresteia**, John Littleworth in **Bartholomew Fair**, Horatio in **Hamlet**, Streaky Bacon in David's Hare's **Racing Demon**, Mole in **Wind in the Willows, The Strangeness of Others**, and Handkes **The Long Way Round**.

TV includes: **Call Me Mister, A Very Peculiar Practice, Poirot, The Bill, The Good Guys, Stalag Luft, Murder Most Horrid, The Chief, Wycliffe,** and Shadwell in **The Buddha of Suburbia,** with Roger Michell.

Films include: **Privates on Parade**, and Rupert the young fogey in Mike Leigh's **High Hopes**. Radio includes Mr Dick in **David Copperfield**

Most recently David played Mr Collins in Andrew Davies' adaptation of **Pride and Prejudice** for the **BBC**.

ANTHONY CALF
(John)
For the Royal Court: **My Night with Reg**.
Other theatre: **The Madness of George III** (Royal National Theatre): **Green Fingers** (Kings Head); **Another Country** (Queens); **Filumena** (Churchill, Bromley); **Godspell** (Northcott, Exeter); **The Boyfriend** (Nottingham Playhouse); **A Midsummer Night's Dream** (New Shakespeare Company).
TV includes: **Bramwell, Pride and Prejudice, Riders, Bye Bye Baby, Absolute Hell, Poirot, Mysteries of the Black Jungle, Dawn and the Candidate, Great Expectations, Tanamera, Mary Rose, My Family and Other Animals, Fortunes of War, Fools on the Hill, The Monocled Mutineer, Drummonds**.
Films include:**The Madness of George III, Gare au Male, Oxford Blues, To Catch a King**.

WILLIAM DUDLEY
(Designer)
For the Royal Court: **Small Change, The Fool, Hamlet, Edmond, Kafka's Dick, Etta Jenks, My Night with Reg**.
For the Royal National Theatre: **Lavender Blue, Larkrise to Candleford, Lost Worlds, The World Turned Upside Down, Spirit of '76, Undiscovered Country, Dispatches, Don Quixote, Schweyk in the Second World War, The Mysteries, The Real Inspector Hound, The Critic, Entertaining Strangers, Waiting for Godot, The Shaughran, Cat on a Hot Tin Roof, The Voysey Inheritance, The Changeling, Bartholomew Fair, The Crucible,**

The Coup, Pygmalion, The Rise and Fall of Little Voice, Johnny on a Spot.
For the RSC: **Ivanov, That Good Between Us, Richard III, The Party, Today, Merry Wives of Windsor, Richard II, A Midsummer Night's Dream**.
Other theatre designs include: **Marya** (Old Vic); **The Ship** (Glasgow Cultural Capital of Europe 1990); **Kiss Me Kate, Girlfriends, Heartbreak House** (West End); **The Deep Blue Sea** (Almeida); **The Big Picnic** (Harland & Wolffs, Glasgow).
Opera designs include: **Anna Christie, Barber of Seville, Idomeneo** (WNO); **Billy Budd** (Metropolitan, New York); **Seraglio** (Glyndebourne); **Tales of Hoffmann, Der Rosenkavalier, Don Giovanni, Cunning Little Vixen** (ROH); **Ring Cycle** (Bayreuth); **Un Ballo in Masquera** (Salzburg Festival); **Lucia di Lammermoor** (Lyric, Chicago); **Lucia di Lammermoor** (Paris National Opera, opening January 1995)
TV includes: **Persuasion** for BBC Television.

JOE DUTTINE
(Eric)
Graduated from the Drama Centre in 1992. For the Royal Court: **My Night With Reg**.
Other theatre includes: **Pondlife** (The Bush); **A Month in the Country** (Watford Palace).
TV includes **Between the Lines, Lovejoy, The Buddha of Suburbia, Pie in the Sky, The Red and The Black, Seaforth, Capital Lives, Touch of Frost**.

ROGER FROST
(Bernie)
For the Royal Court: **The Devil's Gateway, No End of Blame, The Last Supper, Seven Lears, Golgo** (also on tour with all except **Devil's**

Gateway); **My Night With Reg**. Other theatre includes: **Love of a Good Man**, **Psy Warriors**, **The Government Inspector**, **Toad of Toad Hall** (Sheffield Crucible); **Dr. Faustus** (Lyric Hammersmith & West End); **Hamlet** (UK & European Tour); **The Seagull** (Oxford Playhouse & Tour); **A Jovial Crew**, **The Winter's Tale**, **Anthony and Cleopatra**, **The Merry Wives of Windsor** (RSC). TV includes: **Eastenders**, **Pity in History**, **Much Ado About Nothing**, **Teddy Bears Picnic**, **The Monocled Mutineer**, **A Sense of Guilt**, **Imaginary Friends**, **Adrian Mole**, **The Bill**, **Bergerac**, **Inspector Morse**, **The Grass Arena**, **Witchcraft**, **Lovejoy** & **Milner**. Films: **Time Bandits**, **Deadly Advice** & **Young Poisoners Handbook.**

JON LINSTRUM
(Lighting Designer)
For the Royal Court: **Thyestes**, **My Night with Reg**, **Weldon Rising**, **Marching for Fausa**.
Other recent credits include: **Grand Duchess of Gerolstein** (Scottish Opera) **The Life of The World to Come** (Almeida); **Get off My Foot**, **Dr Faustus** (Nottingham Playhouse); **Party Girls**, **It's a Great Big Shame!**, **One Step Beyond**, **Worlds Apart**, **A Night in Tunisia**, (Stratford East); **Hunchback of Notre Dame** (West Yorkshire Playhouse); **The Last Yankee** (Leicester Haymarket) **A Midsummer Night's Dream** (Edinburgh Lyceum); **Lion in the Streets** (Hampstead); **Women in Mind**, **Private Lives**, **Duet For One**, **Salsa Celestina** (Watford Palace); **Rosmersholm** (Young Vic); **The Knickers** and **No Remission**, (Lyric, Hammersmith); and many shows for the Queens Theatre Hornchurch including: **It's Now or Never**, **Aladdin**, **Pump Boys and Dinettes**, **An Evening with Gary Lineker.**
In the West End - **Waiting for Godot**

(Queen's Theatre); **Silly Cow**, **John Sessions' Travelling Tales** (Theatre Royal Haymarket); Jon has worked extensively with Kenneth Branagh's Renaissance Theatre Company lighting **Look Back in Anger** (Belfast and London); **Twelfth Night** (Riverside Studios); John Sessions' **Napoleon the American Story** (Phoenix) **King Lear** and **Midsummer Night's Dream** (World Tour).

KENNETH MACDONALD
(Benny)
For the Royal Court: **Babies**, **My Night with Reg**.
Other theatre includes: **It Ain't Half Hot Mum**, (Scarborough and Bournemouth); **A Midsummer Night's Dream** (Bedford Theatre Co,); **The Day War Broke Out** (Sheffield Crucible and Bush); **Macbeth** (Shaw); **The Second Mrs Tanqueray**, **Jack and The Beanstalk** (Lyceum Crewe); **Say Goodnight to Grandma** (Belgrade); **A Day in the Death of Joe Egg**, **Hadrian VII**, **A Touch of Purple** (Leatherhead); **Animal Farm** (Royal National Theatre); **The Cheekie Chappie** (Regional Tour); **Ladybird** (Hyman and Kass tour); **Private Times** (Library Theatre).
TV includes: **Only Fools and Horses**, **It Ain't Half Hot Mum**, **Last of the Summer Wine**, **Dad's Army**, **Come Back Mrs Noah**, **The Dick Emery Show**, **The Cilla Black Show**, **Softly Softly**, **Z Cars**, **Tenko**, **One by One**, **Games Without Frontiers**, **Silas Marner**, **Chance of a Lifetime**, **Keep an Eye on Albert**, **Farmers Arms**, **Crimewatch**, **Brush Strokes**, **The Chain**, **The Famous Five**, **Upstairs Downstairs**, **Shine on Harvey Moon**, **Surgical Spirit**, **Brookside**, **Capital Lives**.
Films include: **Mixed Doubles**, **The Class of Miss McMichael**, **Hitch in Time**, **Breaking Glass**, **Singleton's Pluck**.

ROGER MICHELL

(Director)

Roger Michell first worked at the Royal Court in 1978. He was Assistant Director to John Osborne, Samuel Beckett and Max Stafford-Clark before directing a number of plays and readings in the Theatre Upstairs.

For six years he was at the RSC where his work included **Some Americans Abroad** (which he also directed on Broadway), **Two Shakespearian Actors**, **Restoration**, **Hamlet**, **The Merchant of Venice**, **The Dead Monkey**, **Constant Couple**, **Kissing the Pope** and **Temptation**. In the West End he has also directed **Private Dick**, Old Vic, **Marya,** and at the Royal National Theatre **The Coup**. Since 1991 he has directed two serials for BBC2; **Downtown Lagos,** and **The Buddha of Suburbia** which he co-adapted with Hanif Kureishi. He is currently completing his first feature film, an adaptation by Nick Dear of Jane Austen's **Persuasion**.

JOHN SESSIONS

(Daniel)

For the Royal Court: **Court in the Act** (one man benefit performance 1993); **My Night With Reg**.

Other theatre includes: **Tartuffe** (Playhouse); **Die Fledermaus** (ROH); **Common Pursuit** (Phoenix); **Orton Diaries** (Royal National Theatre); **The Relapse** (Chichester Festival); **The Alchemist** (Lyric, Hammersmith); **Man is Man** (Almeida); **Candy Kisses** (Bush); **Hamlet** (Sheffield Crucible); **A Midsummer Night's Dream, Chameleon Blue** (Liverpool Everyman); **One Flew Over the Cuckoo's Nest** (Manchester Royal Exchange); **Waiting for Godot** (Young Vic); **Limbo Tales** (Gate). Numerous solo shows include; **Travelling Tales** (Haymarket and Tour); **The American Napoleon** (Birmingham Rep and tour, Phoenix Theatre); **The Life of Napoleon** (Riverside and Albery); **At the Eleventh Hour** (Donmar Warehouse); **Lives of the Great Composers, Salute to Dr Johnson, John Sessions Christmas Show** (Riverside Studios); Season of Shows (Kings Head, Edinburgh Festival, Young Vic).

TV includes: John Byrne's **Boswell and Johnson's Tour of the Western Isles;** David Edgars **Citizen Locke; Life with Eliza, Jute City, The New Statesman, Ackroyd's Dickens, A Day in Summer, Menace Unseen, Gramsci, Porterhouse Blue, The Madness Museum, Girls on Top, Boon, Tender is the Night, The Cellar Show, After Midnight, A Clip Round the Year, Laugh, I Nearly Paid my Licence Fee, Around Midnight, The Lenny Henry Show, Spitting Image, Whose Line is it Anyway, Tall Tales, Some Enchanted Evening, On the Spot, John Session's New Year Show, Nice Day at the Office, Saturday Night Live, A History of Psychiatry, Saturday Review, Likely Stories** (New series May 1994).

Films include: **The Princess Cariboo** (released August 1994) **The Pope Must Die, Sweet Revenge, Henry V, Castaway, Whoops Apocalypse, Gunbus, The Bounty, The Sender**.

Radio includes: **New Premises, Whose Line is it Anyway**?, **Beachcomber by the Way**, Von Harvath's **Figaro Gets Divorced;** Snoo Wilson's **Poonsh** and **The Good Doctor,** Anthony Burgess in **Hommage to A.B.** by William Boyd John Sessions has just finished writing a screen play for the BBC with Peter Richardson, with whom he will also co-star and is also writing a film in America with Eric Idle for the film company Miramax.

The English Stage Company at the Royal Court Theatre

Since 1956, the Royal Court Theatre has been the home of the English Stage Company. The English Stage Company was formed to bring serious writing back to the stage. The Court's first Artistic Director, George Devine, wanted to create a vital and popular theatre. He encouraged new writing that explored subjects drawn from contemporary life as well as pursuing European plays and forgotten classics. When John Osborne's Look Back In Anger was first produced in 1956 it forced British Theatre into the modern age. But the Court was much more than a home for "Angry Young Men", illustrated by a repertoire that stretched from Brecht to Ionesco, by way of JP Sartre, Marguerite Duras, Wedekind and Beckett.

The ambition to discover new work which was challenging, innovative and also of the highest quality became the fulcrum of the company's course of action. Early Court writers included Arnold Wesker, John Arden, David Storey, Ann Jellicco, NF Simpson and Edward Bond. They were followed by a generation of writers led by David Hare and Howard Brenton, and in more recent years, celebrated house writers have included Caryl Churchill, Timberlake Wertenbaker, Robert Holman and Jim Cartwright. Many of their plays are now regarded as modern classics.

In line with the policy of nurturing new writing, the Theatre Upstairs has mainly been seen as a place for exploration and experiment, where writers learn and develop their skills prior to the demands of the Main stage auditorium. Anne Devlin, Andrea Dunbar, Sarah Daniels, Jim Cartwright, Clare McIntyre, Winsome Pinnock and Martin Crimp have all benefited from this process. The Theatre Upstairs proved its value as a focal point for new work with the production of the Chilean writer Ariel Dorfman's **Death and the Maiden**. More recently talented young writers as diverse as Jonathan Harvey (joint winner of this years John Whiting Award), Adam Pernak, Phyllis Nagy, Biyi Bandele-Thomas, Gregory Motton and Kevin Elyot, have been shown to great advantage in this space.

1991 to 1994 have been record breaking years at the box office with capacity houses for productions of **Top Girls**, **Three Birds Alighting on a Field**, **Faith Healer**, **Death and the Maiden**, **Six Degrees of Separation**, **King Lear**, **Oleanna**, **Hysteria**, **Cavalcaders** and **The Kitchen**. **Death and The Maiden** and **Six Degrees of Separation** won the **Olivier Award for Best Play** in 1992 and 1993 respectively. **Three Birds Alighting on a Field** was awarded **Best West End Play** by the Writer's Guild of Great Britain. **Hysteria** won 1994's **Olivier Award for Best Comedy**.

After nearly four decades the Royal Court's aims remain consistent with those of George Devine. The Royal Court Theatre is still a major focus in the country for the production of new work. Scores of plays first seen in Sloane Square are now part of the national and international dramatic repertoire.

My Night With Reg is the fifth play to transfer to the West End in three years, following **Death and the Maiden**, **Six Degrees of Separation**, **Oleanna** and **The Queen and I**. **My Night with Reg** is the first play to transfer directly from the Theatre Upstairs to the West End since **The Rocky Horror Show**.

FOR THE ROYAL
COURT THEATRE

Artistic Director
Stephen Daldry

General Manager
Graham Cowley

Finance Administrator
Mark Rubinstein

Associate Directors
Elyse Dodgson
James Macdonald
Ian Rickson
Max Stafford-Clark

Casting Director
Lisa Makin

Production Manager
Bo Barton

Master Carpenter
Nick Collie

Chief Electrician
Johanna Town

Sound Designer
Paul Arditti

Wardrobe Supervisor
Jennifer Cook

Press
Anne Mayer
(0171 730 2652)

FOR ROYAL COURT THEATRE PRODUCTIONS

DIRECTORS
Stuart Burge CBE
Anthony Burton
Graham Cowley
Harriet Cruickshank
Stephen Daldry

Robert Fox
Sonia Melchett
John Mortimer CBE QC
Alan Rickman
Max Stafford-Clark

General Management
Graham Cowley

Mark Rubinstein

Assisted by
Catherine King

Rachel Harrison

Marketing
Guy Chapman for Chapman Duncan Associates
(0171 242 1882)

Press
Peter Thompson Associates (0171 436 5991)

BILL KENWRIGHT

Royal Court Theatre Productions is pleased to present My Night with Reg in association with Bill Kenwright. His recent West End productions include **Only the Lonely**; **The Miracle Worker**; Harold Pinter's **No Man's Land** and his new play **Moonlight**; **The Deep Blue Sea**; **Present Laughter**; **The Winslow Boy**; **Travels with my Aunt**; **Dancing at Lughnasa**; **Medea** (West End and Longacre Theatre New York). Directed by Peter Hall: **An Ideal Husband**; **An Absolute Turkey**; **The Gift of the Gorgon**; **Lysistrata** (Athens and West End); **Separate Tables**; **She Stoops to Conquer**; **Plaf** and **On Approval**. Willy Russell's **Blood Brothers** is in its seventh year at the Phoenix Theatre and its second year at the Music Box Theatre, New York. He is the controller of the Thorndike Theatre, Leatherhead and the Liverpool Playhouse. He has recently received an Honorary Doctorate from the Liverpool John Moores University.

For Bill Kenwright Limited

Managing Director
Bill Kenwright

Associate Producer
Simon Meadon

Chief Executive
Brett Finnigan

Production Administrator
Max Finbow

Director of Production
Lucille J. Wagner

Production Manager
David Edwards

The Producers of My Night With Reg wish to acknowledge financial support received from The Theatre Investment Fund, a registered charity, which invests in many commercial productions, funds seminars for new producers and raises money for the commercial theatre. If you love the Theatre and wish to promote its future, please consider making a gift to the Fund. For further information regarding the Fund and its activities, please contact:
Chief Executive, Theatre Investment Fund Limited, The Palace Theatre, Shaftesbury Avenue, W1V8AY. Telephone 0171 287 2144

THE AUDREY SKIRBALL-KENIS PLAYWRIGHTS PROGRAMME

Since it began in 1956, the aim of the English Stage Company has always been to develop and perform the best in new writing for the stage. In our present climate it is more important than ever for the Royal Court to adhere to these principles of development which have proved so successful in the past. **The Audrey Skirball-Kenis Playwrights Programme at the Royal Court** allows us to expand this work.

The **Audrey Skirball-Kenis Theatre** is a non-profit arts service organisation based in Los Angeles. Since its founding in 1989 the ASK Theatre has sought to contribute to the quality, growth and vitality of theatre through the development of new writing for the stage. This mandate is being accomplished by offering comprehensive programmes and support services which provide direct assistance to playwrights. The Audrey Skirball-Kents Playwrights Programme at the Royal Court is unique in its transatlantic connection. Through combinations of workshops, readings, dramaturgy, productions without decor and commissioning, this new and creative programme will provide the opportunity for generations of writers to share their innovative ideas, aesthetics and working methods. In doing so these aims will not only benefit the programme of work presented at the Royal Court in the future, but also nourish contemporary theatre, nationally and internationally.

The English Stage Company at the Royal Court Theatre receives funding from:
Arts Council of England, London Boroughs Grants Committee and The Royal Borough of Kensington and Chelsea.
It is the recipient of a grant from the Theatre Restoration Fund and from the Foundation for Sport and the Arts.
Its principal sponsors are: Barclays Bank, Marks & Spencer, British Gas North Thames, the Audrey Skirball-Kenis Theatre, The Rayne Foundation, Sir John Cass' Foundation, The Jerwood Foundation.
Registered Charity Number 231242

The Criterion Theatre

In 1870, following the acquisition of the White Bear Inn site and adjoining properties between Jermyn Street and Piccadilly Circus, caterers Spiers and Pond commissioned Thomas Verity to prepare a scheme for a new development consisting of a large restaurant, dining rooms and galleried concert hall. Having commenced building work it was decided to alter the proposed concert hall (retaining however the composers' names lining the tiled staircase) to a theatre, which opened in 1874. Being underground and lit by gas, essential fresh air had to be mechanically pumped into the auditorium to prevent the audience being asphyxiated - making the area into one of the earliest air conditioned environments in London. From 1879 to 1899 the Criterion was run by actor/manger Charles Wyndham, who gained the theatre a reputation for light comedy with many of the productions starring his wife, Mary Moore. In between the war years notable events included John Gielgud appearing in Musical Chairs and in 1936 a three year run of French Without Tears launched the career of Terence Rattigan. During World War II the underground auditorium made an ideal broadcast studio for the BBC. From 1945 the repertoire included more avant garde works with Beckett's Waiting For Godot (1955), Anouilh's The Waltz Of The Toreadors (1956) - both directed by Peter Hall, Alan Ayckbourn's Absurd Person Singular (1973), Bent (1978) and Dario Fo's Can't Pay Won't Pay (1981) amongst others. Reopened in

October 1992, and having undergone major refurbishment back and front of house, the Criterion retains an almost perfectly preserved Victorian auditorium with an intimacy and atmosphere that makes the building a pleasure both to visit and to work in.

The Criterion Theatre is a perfect venue for conferences, corporate training, press and product launches. For information on hiring the theatre please contact :
Fiona Callaghan on 0171 839 8811.

For the Criterion Theatre

Director Sally Greene	Chief Electrician Simon Thomas
General Manager Bob Eady	Box Office Manager Ken Paul (0171 839 4488)
Financial Controller Bob Findlay	Stage Door Keeper David Harrison
Operations Manager Fiona Callaghan	Head of Bars Lynda Wilson

In accordance with the requirements of the council:

Persons shall not be permitted to stand or sit in any of the gangways intersecting the seating, or to sit in any of the other gangways. If standing be permitted in the gangways at the sides and rear of the seating, it shall be limited to numbers included in the notices exhibited in those positions.

THE SAFETY CURTAIN MUST BE LOWERED AND RAISED IN THE PRESENCE OF EACH AUDIENCE

MY NIGHT WITH REG

For

MICHAEL BURLINGTON
(1949-1985)

and

ANDREI TOOTH
(1950-1987)

'By eight o'clock all was over, and nothing remained
except darkness as on any other night, always.'

Giuseppe di Lampedusa, *The Leopard,*
translated by Archibald Colquhoun

Characters

JOHN – mid-30s.

GUY – mid-30s.

ERIC – 18.

DANIEL – mid-30s.

BERNIE – mid-40s.

BENNY – late 30s.

Setting

Guy's flat. Ground floor. Sitting-room. A conservatory adjoins it leading into the garden. A door leads into the rest of the flat.

NB: Eric hails from Bradford, of which Odsal Top, Whetley Hill and Buttershaw are suburbs. I once thought he might come from Birmingham. In homage to my hometown, this is the place referred to in the printed text.

A few minor changes have been made to the script as performed.

K.E.

Scene One

*'Every Breath You Take' by The Police starts playing. As
the lights come up, the music fades. Late afternoon. Cloudy.
ERIC is painting a window-frame in the conservatory. He's
listening to a walkman. JOHN and GUY are standing in the
sitting-room. GUY is wearing an apron.*

JOHN. Am I early?

GUY. No.

JOHN. I couldn't remember what time you said.

GUY. You're not, really.

> JOHN *glances at the apron.* GUY *suddenly remembers he's
> wearing it.*

> (*Taking it off.*) I was just stiffening some egg whites.

JOHN. You look well.

GUY. Do I?

JOHN. Yes.

GUY. I've been to Lanzarote.

JOHN. Oh.

GUY. You look well, too.

JOHN. Thanks.

GUY. You don't look a day older.

JOHN. Well –

GUY. You don't, honestly. You're just the same.

JOHN. It's been a year or two, hasn't it?

GUY. Nine-and-a-half, actually.

JOHN. God!

GUY. When we passed each other on the escalator at Camden
Town.

JOHN. Yeah.

GUY. I'm so surprised to see you.

ERIC (*singing along with his tape*). 'Baby, baby, please . . . '

GUY. He was supposed to have finished yesterday.

JOHN. I've got the right day, haven't I?

GUY. Oh yes. It's just that when I phoned, it sounded like you weren't going to be able to make it. I'm really pleased you have. Would you like a drink?

JOHN. Scotch. Thanks.

GUY *shoves the apron in a drawer on his way to the drinks table.*

GUY. Anything with it?

JOHN. As it comes.

GUY. Ice?

JOHN. No.

GUY. Straight?

JOHN. Yes.

GUY. Right.

He pours two scotches.

JOHN. Is it one of the Balearics?

GUY. What?

JOHN. Lanzarote.

GUY. Canaries.

JOHN. Oh.

GUY. But I know what you mean. Sort of interchangeable, aren't they?

JOHN. Was it fun?

GUY. Yes. Well, sort of.

He hands him a drink.

JOHN. Cheers!

GUY. Cheers!

They drink.

I've got a bit of bad news, actually.

JOHN. Have you?

GUY. I'm afraid Daniel's had to cry off at the last minute. I'd have let you know, but as it seemed unlikely you were going to come –

JOHN. It's okay. I know.

GUY. Do you?

JOHN. I bumped into Reg last night. At a film.

GUY. Oh.

JOHN. He's gone to Sydney, hasn't he?

GUY. Yes. Some sheep-farmer reckons he's found a Pissarro in his shed. At least, Daniel thinks that's what he said. So you don't mind?

JOHN. No.

GUY. Good. It'd have been fun, though, wouldn't it? The three of us together after all this time. You don't feel you're here under false pretences, then?

JOHN. Of course not. Why should I?

GUY. Well, Daniel's your old mate, isn't he? You've kept in touch –

JOHN. On and off.

GUY. Whereas we . . . How was the film?

JOHN. It wasn't up to much. Two hours of French people talking. I couldn't see the point.

GUY. What was it?

ERIC (*singing with his tape*). 'I'll be watching you . . . '

GUY. Would you like a nut?

JOHN. I'm okay, thanks.

GUY. No, I meant to put them out.

*He goes out. JOHN glances at ERIC. GUY enters with a
bowl of nuts which he puts on the coffee-table.*

Help yourself.

JOHN (*taking out a packet of cigarettes*). Do you?

GUY. No.

JOHN. Do you mind if I do?

GUY. Not at all. I'll find the ashtray.

*He goes out again as JOHN lights a cigarette and looks
round. GUY returns with an ashtray.*

Anyway, Reg is still coming, so . . . He's not exactly the life
and soul, but I sort of like him. Do you?

JOHN. Yeah.

GUY. And they seem very happy together. What did he make of
the film?

JOHN. I'm not sure. It's a nice flat.

GUY. Do you think so?

JOHN. Yes.

GUY. I must say, I'm really quite pleased with it. In fact, I was
thinking the other night, I don't see why I should ever have to
move again.

JOHN. I could never think that.

GUY. You're not the settling type though, are you? Well, you
weren't. Sit down, please.

JOHN. You don't have to be polite, you know.

GUY. No. Sorry.

JOHN flops into an armchair.

You always used to do that.

JOHN. What?

GUY. Sort of hurl yourself at furniture.

JOHN. Oh, I'm sorry –

GUY. No, no . . . it's just . . . seeing it again . . .

ERIC (*singing with his tape*). 'I feel so cold and I long for your embrace . . .'

GUY (*sidling towards the conservatory*). Eric.

No response.

Eric.

ERIC (*lifting his earphones*). Eh?

GUY. How's it going?

ERIC. Done in a tick.

GUY. Only it's getting on . . .

He replaces his earphones and carries on. Meanwhile, JOHN's been fidgeting in his chair. He feels behind a cushion and produces a long, tubular piece of knitting. GUY clocks this.

GUY. Oh –

JOHN. I thought I felt something.

GUY (*taking it off him*). Sorry.

JOHN. What is it?

GUY (*putting it in a drawer*). A cover for my door-sausage, actually.

JOHN. Oh.

Beat.

Do you do a lot of knitting?

GUY. No. Well, from time to time. I find it quite therapeutic.

JOHN. Really?

GUY. A sort of lust-depressant.

JOHN. Why would you need that?

GUY. Well . . . with things as they are . . .

JOHN. You haven't given it up, have you?

GUY. No, no. I think it's given me up, to tell you the truth. But one does need to be careful. Don't you think? You didn't mind me ringing, did you?

JOHN. No.

GUY. Only I remember Daniel saying you'd popped round for dinner some months ago and, as I was having this little do, I thought it'd be nice if you came, so I got your number off him. I was quite surprised to get you. Daniel said you've been difficult to get hold of recently. He thought you may have gone away.

JOHN. No. I've been around. But I'm not that clever at keeping in touch.

GUY. He said you weren't – disappearing for a few years, then suddenly reappearing on the doorstep.

JOHN. Yeah.

GUY. So what have you been up to?

JOHN. In what way?

GUY. Any way, really.

JOHN. Travelled a bit, hung around a bit. Fuck-all, actually. And you?

GUY. Oh, plodding along . . . as you do . . .

Beat.

JOHN. I was thinking . . . on my way over . . .

GUY. Yes?

JOHN. That play we did for DramSoc –

GUY. 'The Bacchae'?

JOHN. Yes.

GUY. Christ!

JOHN. It was good.

GUY. Did you think so?

JOHN. Well . . . it was a laugh.

GUY. You were ever so good as Dionysus.

JOHN. Oh . . .

GUY. No, you were. Especially as it was your first role.

JOHN. And last! That bloody jock-strap you made me do it in! My balls kept falling out.

GUY. Oh, yes . . .

He sips his drink.

JOHN. And the chorus! Finished me every night. All those Danny La Rues miming to a tape.

GUY. Marlene Dietrichs, actually.

JOHN. Were they?

GUY. A Classics professor thought it was 'truly Euripidean'.

JOHN. Daniel thought it was crap. Wrongly, in my opinion.

GUY. That was sour grapes. He was so cross I didn't give him Agave.

JOHN. I'd forgotten that.

GUY. It was such a coup getting you.

JOHN. Why?

GUY. Well, you know . . . Do you still play rugby?

JOHN. No.

GUY. You look fit.

JOHN. That's because I go to the gym. I can't face getting old.

GUY. You're not old. None of us are.

ERIC (*singing with his tape*). 'I hope my legs don't break . . . '

JOHN *glances at* ERIC.

GUY. We're not.

JOHN (*referring to his glass*). Could I?

GUY. Please.

He takes the glass to the drinks table.

JOHN. I'll go and get some. I forgot.

GUY. There's no need to. I've got loads.

JOHN. No, I will.

GUY. There's no need, really. So what are you actually up to now? Workwise.

JOHN. Nothing much. Well, nothing at all. I'm not sure I see the point if you don't have to.

GUY. Of course, your father died, didn't he?

JOHN. Yeah, and Mum died a few years ago.

GUY. I'm sorry.

JOHN. Just in time, really, cos I'd nearly got through what Dad left me.

GUY. Oh.

He hands him a drink.

Cheers!

JOHN. Cheers!

He drinks.

I sometimes think about investing in a pub . . . or a restaurant, maybe.

GUY. You need something, don't you?

JOHN. I dabbled in sports gear for a while. Ages ago. But I couldn't get into it. Got a bit restless. Of course now I've got a stake in the Holland Park pad. We'll probably sell it; it's too big for me, and my brother and sister don't want it: they're both very respectably married and into heavy breeding. They see me as the family reprobate.

GUY. Do they?

JOHN. Which I am. And what about you, workwise?

GUY. Oh, it's not very interesting. I did a bit of this and that and ended up as a copywriter, which is what I still am. Well, you probably know through Daniel.

JOHN. Yeah . . . And what about the sentimental side of things?

GUY. The odd near-miss. I thought we might eat outside.

JOHN. It's going to piss down.

GUY. Daniel mentioned you'd met someone.

JOHN. Did he?

GUY. Yes. An air-steward?

JOHN. Oh! That was way back. He pissed off with a pilot. I don't know why I bothered. I fucking hate air-stewards at the best of times; false tans, false smiles, wiggling their bottoms in everyone's face.

GUY. And that's before they get on the plane.

JOHN laughs. ERIC looks round. They drink.

JOHN. So do you enjoy living alone?

GUY. Yes. Do you?

JOHN. Yes.

Beat.

Guy?

GUY. What?

Beat.

JOHN. I'll go and get a bottle.

GUY. No, don't. There's plenty. Really.

Beat. JOHN lights a cigarette as ERIC appears at the conservatory entrance.

ERIC. Got any turps?

GUY. Turps. Yes.

He goes out.

ERIC. Only I left in a bit of a rush. Forgot me rags an' all.

Beat.

JOHN. What you listening to?

ERIC. The Police.

JOHN. Oh.

ERIC. D'you like them?

JOHN. I think I did . . .

ERIC. They're great.

Beat.

JOHN. Birmingham?

ERIC. How did you know?

JOHN. Been down here long?

ERIC. Six months nearly. I live with my aunty.

Beat.

I don't see her much. (*Re. the conservatory.*) Nice, isn't it?

JOHN. Yes.

ERIC. I've painted all this, you know.

Enter GUY with turps.

GUY. That's it, I'm afraid.

ERIC. Ta.

GUY. Would you like a drink?

ERIC. Not while I'm on the job. But thank you for asking.

He returns to the conservatory, replaces his earphones and starts clearing up.

GUY. He's a bit slow, but very good. There's nothing he can't put his hand to. It's quite a small do. I hope you don't get bored.

JOHN. Course I won't.

GUY. It's funny – glancing through the names in my address-book, I realised I didn't like most of them and the ones I did like had either split up or died . . . well, one of them had. Of the ones who'd split up, I couldn't decide which partner to invite and the dead friend . . . she was no problem at all, so we're down to five. Apart from us two and Reg, there'll be Benny and Bernie. You won't know them. Neither does Reg. Daniel's met them a few times, but . . . I met them at The Frog and Trumpet, where Eric works part-time. In fact, they put me onto him. Bernie's quite nice. A bit odd, mind you. He sells plastic cups. I think you'll like Benny, though. He drives a bus. It's more of a token gathering, but I thought it'd be nice to . . . wet the baby's head, so to speak. My little flat. It's such a shame Daniel can't make it.

JOHN. Yeah.

GUY. God, the two of you!

JOHN. A bit out of order, weren't we?

GUY. It never seemed to stop.

JOHN. Should've graduated in shafting. I might have got a First, then.

GUY. And the rivalry! Whoever you had, Daniel had to have, and vice versa.

JOHN. Yeah.

GUY. Anyway . . .

Beat.

Would you like to see the garden?

The doorbell rings.

(*Looking at his watch.*) I don't believe it!

JOHN. I knew I'd got it wrong.

GUY. No, no, you haven't. Honestly.

He goes out. JOHN gets up and checks himself in a mirror. The sound of the front door being opened.

(*Off.*) Daniel!

JOHN freezes.

DANIEL (*off*). Gert!

GUY (*off*). You're supposed to be in Sydney.

DANIEL (*off*). I know!

GUY (*off*). Guess who's here!

DANIEL bursts in with a bag. JOHN opens his arms.

JOHN. Dan!

DANIEL. Juanita!

They embrace extravagantly. ERIC clocks this.

What the fuck are you doing here? Don't tell me – you got the time wrong.

JOHN. I knew I had.

GUY. You haven't.

DANIEL. Very early, very late or very absent! You old pouf!

JOHN. Not old!

They embrace again. DANIEL mauls JOHN's backside.

DANIEL. Darling, it's dropped!

JOHN. Fuck off!

DANIEL. Dropped, dropped, dropped! At least two inches! It'll
be dragging on the floor before the night's out.

*JOHN tweaks one of DANIEL's nipples. DANIEL shrieks.
ERIC looks on.*

No, it hasn't! It's perfect! I promise!

JOHN lets go.

The Flying Fuck of the First Fifteen!

They embrace again.

Darling, be gentle! I'm still intacta.

JOHN. How are you?

DANIEL. Earthbound. The plane wouldn't work. Why haven't
you phoned?

JOHN. You know what I'm like.

DANIEL. It's months. You promised faithfully. (*To* GUY.) It's a
miracle he's here. (*Extending an arm to* GUY.) Gertie!

GUY goes to DANIEL, who puts his arms round them both.

The Beverleys live! I've got just the thing.

He goes to his bag and clocks ERIC.

(*Mouthing.*) Who is that?

GUY. Eric.

DANIEL (*mouthing*). To die!

*He takes a bottle of champagne from his bag and starts to
open it.*

Gertie, get the glasses! Warm as shit, but fuck it!

GUY *grabs three glasses.*

(*Re.* ERIC.) Would your friend like some?

GUY. He's busy.

The cork pops and champagne sprays.

DANIEL (*to* JOHN). Always reminds me of you.

He starts pouring.

Hideously naff to do it like that, but why drink it if you don't flaunt it?

JOHN. I ought to get some.

GUY. There's no need.

DANIEL. Don't tell me! You forgot to bring a bottle. Quelle surprise! Well, at least you got the right address.

JOHN *cuffs his ear.*

Ow! (*Raising his glass.*) Gross indecency!

JOHN & GUY. Gross indecency!

They drink.

GUY. I can't believe this. We were just saying what a shame you couldn't be here. Actually, why are you here?

DANIEL (*singing*). 'Didn't know what time it was, the lights were low-oh-oh, I leaned back on my radio-oh-oh . . . '

JOHN *picks it up.*

DANIEL & JOHN. 'Some cat was layin' down some rock'n'roll, lotta soul, he said . . . '

DANIEL (*con emozione*). 'There's a starman waiting in the sky . . . '

JOHN. You've skipped a bit.

DANIEL (*regardlessly*). 'He'd like to come and meet us . . . '

JOHN *rejoins. Also* GUY, *tentatively.*

DANIEL, JOHN & GUY. 'But he thinks he'd blow our minds, There's a starman waiting in the sky . . . '

DANIEL (*refilling their glasses*). This is heaven on a stick. My little playmates! (*Raising his glass.*) Sodomy!

JOHN & GUY. Sodomy!

They drink.

DANIEL. Colston Hall!

JOHN. Jesus!

DANIEL. You were with Freddie –

JOHN. No, you were with Freddie. I was with Barry.

DANIEL. No, I was with Barry. We'd done a swap. I was with Freddie the night before.

JOHN. Were you?

DANIEL (*to* GUY). Who were you with?

GUY. I was in the gallery. We could only get two pairs and a single –

DANIEL. Then we all went on to the Moulin Rouge –

JOHN. And you lost a contact lens!

DANIEL. That's right!

GUY. And you brought the club to a halt crawling around on all fours in your Ziggy gear –

DANIEL. And I found it in my gin-and-tonic!

JOHN. Jesus!

DANIEL (*singing*). 'If we can sparkle he may land toni-i-ight . . . '.

GUY. But why aren't you in Sydney?

DANIEL. We were stuck on the runway for three hours, then shoved into an hotel that made Treblinka seem like paradise with the promise of a morning take-off. But when I woke up, I thought fuck this for a game of old fairies, got myself on a flight this evening and popped back home to give Reg the most gorgeous surprise which, of course, I did. He was like a startled rabbit and up me before I'd grounded my Gucci. What am I like? It's nearly a year and I'm still besotted. (*To* JOHN.) You've got that look about you.

JOHN. What do you mean?

DANIEL. Don't you think, Guy? I could always tell when you'd been at it. Have you just left a trick panting for more?

JOHN. Have I fuck!

DANIEL. You can't fool me. You have the most lingering post-coital glow of anyone I know. It's absolutely unmistakable. At university, you were glowing for three solid years.

GUY. You both were.

DANIEL. I bet my bippy you've had it off in the past twenty-four hours.

JOHN. I wish I had, but believe it or not, I do occasionally do other things. Like seeing my accountant who's just spent the past few hours giving me a gentle bollocking.

GUY. And going to the cinema. You were there last night, weren't you?

JOHN. That's right.

GUY. Reg can vouch for it.

DANIEL. Reg?

JOHN. We bumped into each other.

DANIEL. Really?

JOHN. Yeah.

DANIEL. He never said. Mind you, we didn't talk much. Major rogering, then he had to piss off. What the fuck were you doing at a Rohmer retrospective? I thought you only liked films with naked men and gratuitous violence.

JOHN. I do. It bored my bum off.

GUY. How long have you got?

DANIEL. About forty years, God willing!

He checks his watch and goes to his bag.

(*Mouthing – re.* ERIC.) Gorgeous!

He takes out a gift and gives it to GUY.

Happy flatwarming, pet!

He kisses him.

GUY (*opening it*). Thank you. (*Taking out a glossy hardback.*) 'Solo Banquets'. You are sweet.

He kisses DANIEL.

DANIEL. Not that you need it; you're the best cook I know. But look who wrote it.

GUY. Gertrude Pinner. (*Laughing.*) Daniel!

DANIEL. And look at the back.

GUY *does so.*

She's doing something ferocious with a meringue and a pile of kumquats.

GUY. Shit! The egg whites! Oh, they'll have to wait.

JOHN. Is that my fault?

GUY. Of course not.

DANIEL. It's bound to be. I don't know what you're talking about, but it's bound to be.

JOHN *cuffs him again.*

Would you stop that? I'll get Reg onto you.

GUY. I'm afraid I haven't got any more champagne, but I think I've got most other things.

JOHN. I wouldn't mind another scotch.

DANIEL. I'll have whatever the big boys are having.

GUY *prepares three scotches.*

(*To* JOHN.) So what've you been up to? Don't tell me – counting the wrinkles, trying to shed a few years at the gym and squandering the family fortune. The idle rich!

JOHN. You can talk!

DANIEL. Some of us have to work. We're not all Harriet Inheritance.

GUY *distributes the drinks.*

JOHN. Cheers!

GUY. Cheers!

DANIEL. Indecent exposure!

JOHN & GUY. Indecent exposure!

They drink.

DANIEL. Are you cooking something simply sensational?

GUY. It's nothing much.

DANIEL. You're the only person I know who could do a Sunday roast on a Baby Belling.

JOHN. You made us some great meals.

GUY. Someone had to feed you. Beans and beer were all you ever seemed to have. Foodwise.

DANIEL. I wish I could stay. Who else is coming?

GUY. Just Benny and Bernie.

DANIEL. Treat in store! Bernie redefines boredom –

GUY. He's not that bad.

DANIEL. Completely barking, but Benny! The Dick of Death!

JOHN. How do you know?

DANIEL. Impossible not to. You could tell his religion through a kaftan. That man is awash with testosterone. And you should see him drive his bus! I had the misfortune to be on it once. Never again! I was sitting on top, screaming.

JOHN. Wouldn't be the first time.

DANIEL (*hitting him*). Harlot!

The phone rings. DANIEL *instantly answers it.*

James Pringle reception. Can I help you?

GUY. Daniel!

DANIEL. Yes, he is. Who shall I say's calling? . . . Oh! (*Passing the phone to* GUY.) It's Brad.

GUY. Hello . . . It's a bit difficult at the moment . . . Have you? . . . I'll phone later, alright? . . . Bye.

He replaces the receiver.

Drinks alright?

DANIEL. So that was Brad, eh?

GUY. Yeah.

DANIEL. Sounded a bit breathy to me.

GUY. Did he?

JOHN. Who's Brad?

GUY. He's no-one.

DANIEL. Come on, Gert!

GUY. Daniel!

DANIEL. They talk to each other. Over the phone.

JOHN. Talk to each other?

DANIEL. You know.

JOHN. Like dirty?

DANIEL. Would you say dirty, Gertie?

GUY. No. Well, yes. Filthy, actually, but there's more to it than that. Well, a bit more. He lives in Theydon Bois.

DANIEL. I've heard it's charming.

GUY. A lorry-driver, so he says. I suspect he's a florist, but what's it matter?

JOHN. Have you met him?

GUY. No. Probably never will. Would you like a top-up?

JOHN. What do you talk about?

GUY. Nothing, really.

DANIEL. Gert!

GUY. Daniel, please!

DANIEL. Brad wants to be housetrained.

JOHN. Housetrained?

GUY. Daniel!

JOHN. How can you housetrain him over the phone?

GUY (*to* DANIEL). You bastard!

DANIEL. Do share!

GUY. I just tell him what to do and he does it, alright?

JOHN. Like what?

GUY. I don't want to talk about it.

JOHN. And how do you know he's doing what you've told him to?

GUY. I don't. But I do hear a lot of panting and he has been known to let out the occasional bark.

JOHN *and* DANIEL *burst out laughing.*

It's a fantasy, for Christ's sake! I'm not entering him for Crufts.

DANIEL (*putting his arm round* GUY). Darling, don't be cross! You know we love you. And I must say, you're looking gorgeous. Isn't he, Jonty? Lampedusa obviously did you the world of good.

GUY. Lanzarote.

DANIEL. That's right. Did you manage to get your end away?

GUY. That's not why I went.

DANIEL. I know, but did you?

GUY. I'm not telling you.

DANIEL. So who was it with?

GUY. Daniel!

DANIEL. He's practically taken the veil, you know.

GUY. I haven't.

DANIEL. He's taking safety to an extreme. You know he masturbates in Marigolds?

GUY. This isn't true –

DANIEL. And he won't look at pornography without a condom over his head.

GUY. I'm just trying to be careful, that's all. And I'm trying not to think about it all the time, which is why I find things to distract me.

JOHN. Like knitting.

DANIEL. And a man who thinks he's a dog.

GUY. I wouldn't expect you to understand. And at least it's safe.

DANIEL. Meanwhile, back in Lanzarote –

GUY. Honestly –

DANIEL. You met this man –

GUY. Daniel –

DANIEL. Mm?

GUY. Well, if you must know . . .

DANIEL. Yes?

GUY. I did.

DANIEL. Oh!

GUY. Only for one night, mind you.

DANIEL. And?

GUY. That's it.

DANIEL. What happened?

GUY. It wasn't very pleasant, actually.

DANIEL. Why not?

GUY. He took advantage of me.

JOHN. How?

GUY. Well, I was a bit drunk, you see, and he forced himself on me. I couldn't do much about it.

JOHN. What a bastard!

GUY. And the worst thing was, he didn't use any protection. Can you imagine? I mean, how irresponsible! I couldn't stop thinking about it. It spoiled the rest of my holiday.

DANIEL. Was he a native?

GUY. No. A mortician from Swindon.

DANIEL *and* JOHN *giggle*.

It isn't funny, Daniel!

DANIEL. Fancy dying in Swindon!

JOHN. Only thing to do there.

GUY. Swindon's hardly the point.

JOHN. When I was at school, we played truant there once. It was so bloody boring, we were back within the hour.

ERIC has appeared at the conservatory entrance.

ERIC. 'Scuse me.

GUY. How are you getting on?

ERIC. No worries. I've just wound my tape back.

GUY. Oh.

ERIC (*to* JOHN). If you wanted to have a listen. Just the first track, like. It's great.

Beat.

JOHN. Okay.

Looks are exchanged between him, DANIEL and GUY, as he goes to ERIC. ERIC leads him into the conservatory and puts the earphones on him. He starts the tape and watches JOHN's reaction. Meanwhile:

GUY. I can't believe he's here! When I asked him, he more or less said no. I nearly died when he turned up. He's just the same, isn't he?

DANIEL. Is he?

GUY. Twelve years! Apart from that time we passed each other in Camden Town. He's exactly as I remember him.

DANIEL. Have you told him you've still got his jockstrap?

GUY. Of course I haven't!

DANIEL. It must be dreadfully rancid by now.

GUY. I can hardly breathe!

DANIEL. Pull yourself together, Gert! It was a post-schoolboy crush. You can't spend the rest of your life lusting after someone you never see.

GUY. I know it's stupid, but . . . You don't really believe me, do you? You don't think it's possible.

DANIEL. And he's hardly reliable. Adorable, but completely irresponsible. The last person to have a relationship with.

GUY. That's not even on the cards.

DANIEL. Then what is on the cards?

GUY. I don't know!

DANIEL. Are you going to tell him?

GUY. No. I can't

DANIEL. Why not? He can only tell you to fuck off or laugh in your face.

GUY. That party!

DANIEL. What party?

GUY. The last night of 'The Bacchae'.

DANIEL. Did I ever tell you how vile I thought it was?

GUY. It was the only time he really talked to me. It wasn't like when the three of us were together. We were sitting up in the flies with a bottle of wine and he just opened up. He talked about everything and then he said something that . . . I just know he was hinting that we should do it and – I don't know why – I hedged around, probably because I was so taken aback. I mean, I was being offered the only thing in the world that I've ever wanted.

DANIEL. And then Pentheus found you and proceeded to puke up, if memory serves. Hardly surprising, considering the production he'd just been in.

GUY. I go over that moment again and again. The biggest regret of my life!

DANIEL. Well, maybe there'll be another moment tonight. You're the host – assert yourself. I doubt you'll end up wed, but if you get him pissed enough, he might let you blow him off behind the Yucca.

JOHN *removes the earphones.*

ERIC. What d'you think?

JOHN. It's nice.

ERIC. D'you like it?

JOHN. Yeah.

ERIC. I told you it was good.

JOHN. Thanks.

ERIC. Cheers.

> ERIC *returns to his clearing up, while* JOHN *returns to the sitting-room.*

DANIEL. Life-changing moment?

JOHN. Quite cute, isn't he?

DANIEL. I'd eat his shit for breakfast. No, I didn't mean that. Well, not really. You are looking at a new man: Monica Monogamy, that's moi. (*To* GUY.) You will look after Reg, won't you? You know he's a bit shy. My little Rinaldo.

GUY. Who?

DANIEL. Reg.

GUY. Rinaldo?

DANIEL. That's his name. Isn't it sweet? But he hates it. Insists on being Anglicised. Well, that's Americans for you. Tell him I love him. Appassionatamente!

GUY. Alright.

DANIEL. The Antipodes beckon.

GUY. I'm so pleased you came.

DANIEL. Gert!

> *They embrace.*

GUY. And thanks for the book.

DANIEL. Major pleasure.

GUY. I hope the sheep-farmer doesn't disappoint you .

DANIEL. If he does, there's always the sheep. And fuck it, it's a trip. Juanita!

> *He embraces* JOHN.

JOHN. It's great to see you again, Dan.

DANIEL. If you don't keep in touch . . .

JOHN. I will. Honestly.

DANIEL. I've never believed a word you've said, but I still adore you.

They kiss.

JOHN. Have a good time!

DANIEL. And you. Both of you.

He picks up his bag and goes to the conservatory entrance.

(*To* ERIC.) Bye!

ERIC. See you.

DANIEL. I think you're doing the most marvellous job.

ERIC. Ta.

DANIEL. My pleasure!

He goes to the door, GUY *following.*

Just one word, Gert.

GUY. What's that?

DANIEL. Yucca!

GUY pushes him out. JOHN lights a cigarette. He and ERIC glance at each other. The sound of the front door being opened.

(*Off.*) I'll phone you when I get back. Happy flatwarming, darling!

GUY (*off*). Bye.

DANIEL (*off*). 'There's a starman waiting in the sky . . . '

GUY (*off*). You'll miss your plane.

DANIEL (*off*). Ciao!

The front door's closed. GUY *re-enters.*

GUY. Well!

JOHN. Look out, Sydney!

GUY. Unbelievable! I mean, just when I was saying what a shame it was the three of us –

JOHN (*re. his glass*). Could I?

GUY (*going to take the glass*). Of course.

JOHN (*going to the drinks table*). It's okay.

He pours a scotch.

Would you like one?

GUY. No. I think I'm alright, thanks.

JOHN. If you want to get on –

GUY. It's fine. All in hand.

JOHN. Don't let me stop you.

GUY. No, it's fine.

JOHN *suddenly covers his face with his hand.*

John?

He seems to be crying.

Are you alright?

ERIC *glances at* JOHN, *then carries on with his work.*

JOHN. Christ, I haven't . . .

GUY. What?

JOHN. For years . . .

GUY. John, what is it?

JOHN. Guy . . .

Beat. Then GUY *goes to him and tentatively puts an arm round him.* JOHN *instantly embraces him, crying freely.* GUY *returns the embrace.*

You're the only one . . . Guy . . . you're the only one . . .

GUY. What are you er . . . ?

JOHN. The only one, Guy . . .

GUY. John . . . ?

JOHN *can't speak for crying.* GUY *doesn't know what's happening. Then he cautiously strokes* JOHN's *hair.*

It's alright . . . (*Getting tearful himself.*) it's alright . . .

He strokes JOHN's *hair more confidently as* JOHN *tries to speak. Then:*

JOHN. Last night . . .

GUY. Yes?

JOHN. Last night . . .

GUY. You were at the pictures.

JOHN. Yeah, and er . . .

GUY. What?

JOHN. Reg . . .

GUY. You bumped into him.

JOHN. Yeah . . . No, I . . .

GUY. You didn't bump into him.

JOHN. No . . . Shit!

GUY. It's okay . . .

JOHN. We met . . .

GUY. Yeah?

JOHN. Like, we meant to . . .

GUY. Yeah?

JOHN. We spent the night together . . .

　　Beat.

　　I haven't cried for years . . . not for years . . .

　　Beat.

GUY. You spent the night together?

JOHN. Yeah . . . Oh, Guy . . . . I love him . . .

GUY. After one night?

JOHN. After nine months –

GUY. Nine months?

JOHN. We've been seeing each other since that dinner-party . . . when we first met . . .

Beat.

You're the only one, Guy . . . the only one I could tell this to.

Beat.

GUY. Oh. I see.

Beat. They gradually get out of the embrace. JOHN *searches his pockets.*

JOHN. Fuck!

GUY (*searching his own pockets*). It's okay.

Finding nothing, he goes to a drawer and pulls out the apron. He hands it to JOHN.

Sorry, it's . . .

JOHN (*taking it and wiping his eyes*). Thank you. I only came because I thought he was in Sydney. He's my best mate. I know I never see him . . . well, hardly ever, but . . . I can't face him.

Beat.

GUY. Then why don't you er . . . you and Reg . . . stop it?

JOHN. We've talked about it, but it's not that easy, Guy . . . when you're in love . . . to let go.

Beat.

GUY. No. I suppose not.

JOHN. You won't tell Reg, will you?

GUY. What?

JOHN. That I've told you. He doesn't want anyone to know. So you won't, will you?

Beat.

GUY. No. Look, I'd better go into the kitchen.

JOHN. Your egg whites.

GUY. Yes . . . and I've got to skim the consommé.

   JOHN *suddenly embraces him tightly.*

JOHN. You're a friend.

Beat.

GUY. Yes.

ERIC*'s standing at the conservatory entrance.*

ERIC. All done.

They look at him. GUY *walks out.*

Have I . . . ?

JOHN. No. So you're not joining us?

ERIC. 'Fraid not. I'm standing in for Eric.

JOHN. Eric?

ERIC. He lets me run it when he's off. He's very good like that.

JOHN. I thought you were Eric.

ERIC. I am. He's the landlord. Frog and Trumpet.

JOHN. Doesn't that get confusing?

ERIC. We've got two Normans an' all.

The sound of banging pans from the kitchen. They register this.

JOHN. Things are working out, then.

ERIC. Sort of. Better than Brum, anyway.

Beat.

I used to stack shelves in Fine Fare.

JOHN. Did you?

ERIC. Then I was a meat-packer in Nechells Green.

Beat.

When I moved down here, I tried to get into security at Marks and Spencer, but they said I didn't have the qualifications.

More banging from the kitchen.

Then my aunty put me in touch with this friend of hers who does interior decorating and I'm managing okay . . .

JOHN. Good.

ERIC. . . . what with The Frog and Trumpet an' all, but what I really want to do is join the police.

JOHN. Are you musical, then?

ERIC. No. I just want to be a policeman.

More banging from the kitchen.

The way they go on in the pub! Can't understand it. They only think about one thing and they don't seem to care much who they do it with, either. I don't want to be like them. There's more to life than that, isn't there?

Beat.

JOHN. Yes.

ERIC. I can wait. I'm quite happy.

GUY *appears, crying.*

JOHN. What's wrong?

GUY. I've run out of vinegar.

JOHN. What?

GUY. I've run out of pissing vinegar.

He's crying helplessly. Beat. JOHN *puts an arm round him.*

JOHN. I'll go and get some. I was going to get some booze anyway.

Beat.

ERIC. Well, I'll be off, then. It's all done.

GUY (*through tears*). Thank you. It's very nice.

ERIC *goes to the door and turns.*

ERIC. Enjoy the party.

He leaves. Beat.

JOHN. Was there any particular vinegar you wanted?

GUY. No. Anything except malt.

JOHN. Right.

GUY. I'm sorry. Must be all the excitement.

JOHN goes to the door.

JOHN. Oh. I forgot.

He takes a smallish bag from his jacket pocket and hands it to GUY.

For your flatwarming.

GUY. You shouldn't have.

JOHN. It's nothing very much . . . at all, really . . .

GUY looks in the bag.

You could save it for later . . .

GUY takes out a paperback.

I'm afraid I didn't get round to wrapping it.

GUY. 'Cooking For One.' Thanks.

JOHN. Just a gesture.

GUY. No. Thank you.

JOHN leaves. GUY wipes his eyes. He goes to the conservatory entrance and looks at it. Then he sits down. He touches the cover of 'Cooking for One'. Beat. He picks up the phone and dials. He waits, then:

Brad? . . . It's Guy. How are you? . . . Fine. Sorry about earlier . . . Yes . . . Anyway, I just felt like a bit of a chat.

The doorbell rings.

Shit! . . . No, I didn't mean you! . . . I've got to go . . . Brad, I'm sorry . . . I'll call you soon . . . Sorry . . .

He replaces the receiver and gets up as rain suddenly starts pelting down onto the conservatory roof. He looks out.

Oh, no!

The doorbell rings again.

Blackout as the rain continues.

Scene Two

Dusk. The rain is still pelting down onto the roof of the conservatory. BERNIE stands at the entrance, inspecting it. BENNY and JOHN are seated. GUY is hovering. All have drinks. A bowl of nuts sits on the coffee-table.

BERNIE. Nice. Very nice. He's a good little worker. This is the year, Benny, for our conservatory. Adds thousands, you know. I saw a very smart one in a magazine. Reasonable, too. Lots of stained glass – not too garish, but not dull, either – and garlands moulded all the way round with the odd cherub and bird dotted here and there. Very smart it was, with a fountain in the middle. Did I show it you, Benny?

BENNY. Yeah.

BERNIE. I like the sound of water. Very relaxing.

A clap of thunder as the rain becomes torrential.

GUY. Nuts?

Beat.

I planned on eating outside.

JOHN lights a cigarette.

BENNY. Could I?

JOHN offers him one and lights it. GUY provides them with a fresh ashtray.

BERNIE. That's your third.

BENNY. Who's counting?

BERNIE. I am. He gave up for two-and-a-half years, you know. Have you ever given up, John?

JOHN. No.

BERNIE. I used to smoke like a chimney as a kid, up until I was about twenty-one, twenty-one-and-a-half or thereabouts. But I asked myself, 'Bernard, is a nicotine hit more important than life itself?' and I had to answer, 'No.' So I stopped there and then. The best decision I've ever made.

GUY. Are everyone's drinks alright?

BENNY. Wouldn't say no.

GUY goes to take his glass.

It's okay. I'll do it.

GUY. Yes, help yourselves. That's best.

BENNY pours himself a drink.

BERNIE. Good job we didn't bring the car.

More thunder as the rain continues.

Funny thing is, Benjamin and I have never been happier – isn't that right, Ben? We see more of each other, find time to do things we'd never done before. I've read more books these past few years than in my whole life! We've been to the cinema – well, once or twice. Of course, with a video . . . In fact, we saw a film only last week at that cinema in erm . . .

BENNY. East Finchley.

BERNIE. That's the one. French thing. People sitting around talking about this and that . . . well, about themselves, really. Quite interesting.

BENNY. You dropped off.

BERNIE. I'd had a hard day.

BENNY. We thought we were going to see 'Robocop'.

BERNIE. Well, if they do insist on changing the programme halfway through the week!

BENNY. I told you it was French.

BERNIE. Why they can't recognise weeks like the rest of us – i.e. beginning on Sunday and ending on Saturday – is beyond me. But the point is, we saw it and we wouldn't have dreamt of going a couple of years ago. We'd have probably found ourselves in a smokey bar, drinking a lot and spending too much. I can't help thinking it's brought us to our senses, made us realise what we've got going for us.

The doorbell rings. JOHN stands up.

GUY. Are you alright?

JOHN. I'm going to the toilet.

He exits.

GUY. I won't be a minute.

GUY exits.

BENNY. Why do you always go on about fucking conservatories?

BERNIE. You'd like one, wouldn't you?

BENNY. There's a time and place.

BERNIE. Talking of which, you might have worn a looser pair of trousers.

BENNY. This is the only suit I've got.

DANIEL enters, followed by GUY. Beat.

DANIEL. Where's John?

GUY. In the loo.

BENNY. Hello, Dan.

He goes to DANIEL and they embrace. Then DANIEL goes to BERNIE and embraces him. He starts crying. BERNIE's unsure how to cope. He pats his back.

BERNIE. Oh dear . . . dear me . . .

For several seconds, the sound of DANIEL sobbing and the rain outside.Then he releases himself from the embrace and dries his eyes.

GUY. Alright?

DANIEL. Yes.

He suddenly retches. GUY darts across to him.

GUY. Dan!

DANIEL breathes deeply.

DANIEL. I'm alright. Really. Could I have a brandy?

BENNY indicates he'll deal with it and pours a brandy.

Oh, Jesus! Nothing in there.

GUY. Maybe you should try and eat a little something.

DANIEL. Was the music alright?

GUY. Of course it was.

DANIEL. He loved it. Never stopped playing it.

GUY. And you bought it me.

DANIEL. That's right.

BENNY gives him a brandy.

Thanks.

He takes a sip.

Oh! Divine! I mustn't stay long, cos of his mother.

GUY. She's not alone?

DANIEL. No, but I said I'd get back.

GUY. I did ask her.

DANIEL. She thought you were very sweet, but she wanted to stay at the flat.

He takes another sip.

He didn't want a funeral, you know, but I couldn't not for her . . . for me . . . I didn't follow his wishes. Pretty appalling, isn't it?

GUY. You did the right thing.

DANIEL. He'd have been furious.

GUY. It's you who has to deal with it. You've done nothing wrong.

The rain has been easing off.

DANIEL. How long's he going to be in there?

GUY. Shall I give him a shout?

DANIEL. He's probably transfixed in front of the mirror. Give him another half-hour.

He has another sip.

I think I'll pop into the garden for a minute. Get a bit of air.

BERNIE. Would you mind if I joined you? Bit smokey, isn't it?

DANIEL. As long as you keep your hands to yourself, Bernard. No funny business in the shrubbery, now!

BERNIE (*unsure how to react*). No . . .

They go into the garden as BENNY *replenishes his glass.*

BENNY. Want anything?

GUY. I'm fine, thanks.

BENNY. I think I'll join them. What about you?

GUY. In a minute. I need to check the food.

BENNY. Right.

He goes into the garden as JOHN *enters.*

GUY. Okay?

JOHN. Yeah.

GUY. They're in the garden.

JOHN. Right. (*Re. his glass.*) May I?

GUY. You know you don't have to ask.

JOHN pours himself a scotch. GUY *sips his drink.*

All pretty difficult, isn't it?

JOHN. You could say that.

GUY. For everyone, really.

JOHN. Mm.

He gulps his drink.

Maybe I should go.

GUY. You can't do that! It'd look so odd. Well . . . I suppose if you want to –

JOHN. No, you're right.

Beat.

GUY. I know it's the wrong time to say this and it's not really my business, but . . . I can't help feeling that, in the long run, it might be easier for you both if you . . . actually got round to

telling him sometime. Obviously not today, but . . . sometime.
I'm speaking out of turn, aren't I? But it seems so unfair . . .
to both of you, not just Daniel. I mean, you're friends, John.
You just can't have that sort of secret and the longer it goes
on . . . I'm sorry.

JOHN. You're right.

GUY. After what you've been through, I really shouldn't . . . I'm
sorry.

Beat.

JOHN. The last time I saw him – it's funny, but I knew it was the
last time . . . One minute – that's all I had. Dan had popped
out the room for some reason or other and . . . Cos the rest of
the time, Dan was at the bedside, holding his hand . . . which
is as it should be, isn't it? And me pretending I was just a
friend. I couldn't even see his fucking corpse.

Enter BENNY.

BENNY. Bernie's so fucking boring sometimes, I don't know
how I've put up with him all these years. He's twittering
on about fuck-knows-what out there. I've had to come in, else
I'd have whacked him with a spade. Sorry, am I interrupting?

GUY. No.

JOHN. I'll be in the kitchen.

JOHN *exits.*

BENNY. I'm not, am I?

GUY. No.

BENNY (*Re. his glass*). May I?

GUY. Of course.

BENNY *replenishes his drink.*

BENNY. What a cunt! Garbage by the fucking yard! But the
funny thing is, I only seem to notice what a complete prick he
can be when other people are around. Want anything?

GUY. I'm fine, thanks.

BENNY. Cheers!

GUY. Cheers!

They drink. BENNY *lights a cigarette.* GUY *gets him an ashtray.*

BENNY. I dunno! Fucking turn-up, isn't it?

GUY. Yeah.

BENNY. Why do they have to play that bloody music? It's upsetting enough as it is.

GUY. It was one of Reg's favourites.

BENNY. He wasn't there to hear it, was he?

GUY. It's difficult knowing what to do. There's no time, everyone's distressed.

BENNY. I want to be put in a bin-liner and chucked out with the rubbish.

GUY. It's the people left behind, though, isn't it?

Beat.

It was funny seeing everyone in suits. Especially when you're used to them in more recherché gear

BENNY. Do you think mine's too tight?

GUY. No.

BENNY. Bernie thinks so. The trousers, anyway.

GUY. It looks fine.

BENNY (*inspecting himself*). I suppose my cock does stick out a bit.

GUY *sips his drink.*

Reg used to love it.

GUY. Italian, isn't it?

BENNY. My cock. Couldn't get enough of it.

He grabs a handful of nuts and starts eating them.

GUY. You had it off with Reg?

BENNY. A few times. Started a couple of years back. At your flatwarming, actually. That's where Bernie and I met him – well, you know that; you introduced us. Made a date for the next night and Bob was your uncle. Cos Daniel was in er . . .

GUY. Sydney.

BENNY. That's the one. He's always somewhere, isn't he? Nice job! Better than the 134, I can tell you!

GUY. I didn't know ...

BENNY. Why should you? No-one does. And Bernie certainly doesn't, so I'd appreciate it if you kept your mouth shut. He's trying to make me a good boy. Thinks we should stay home nights with our feet up. Not really me, though, is it? Don't get me wrong – Bernie and I get on fine. Like a fucking institution after all these years. He'd never leave me.

GUY. Would you leave him?

BENNY. No, but sometimes he gets on my tits. I gotta prowl around a bit, haven't I? Go mad otherwise. Did you like Reg?

GUY. Yes. And he made Daniel happy.

BENNY. He was a good fuck. Bit noisy, though. Not very keen on that; are you? Tends to put me off my stroke. Enjoyed the sound of his own vice, you might say.

He has more nuts.

Between you and me, I thought he was a miserable sod. We never really talked. Just got down to business, then pissed off. But he certainly got my nuts twitching. You don't mind me telling you, do you?

GUY. No.

BENNY. I needed to tell someone and you're the obvious person. I'm pretty fucking worried, I don't mind admitting.

GUY. Did you take any precautions or anything?

BENNY. Of course we did! Sometimes. Well, you didn't really think about that then, did you?

GUY. Some of us did.

BENNY. Every fucking morning, I wake up and check my body, inch by inch, to make sure something hasn't appeared during the night, and when I get back from work, the same routine. And any little cough, twinge or itch brings me out in a cold sweat. And then I start panicking about the fucking cold sweat. I tell you, if I haven't caught anything, it'll be a fucking miracle.

Enter BERNIE.

BERNIE. I was thinking, Guy, it might be possible to eat outside after all.

GUY. Is Daniel alright?

BERNIE. Oh, yes. I've been singing the praises of conservatories, actually. It wouldn't surprise me if he ended up getting one.

BENNY. I don't know where he'd put it. He lives on the top floor.

BERNIE (*re. the glass in his hand*). And he said he'd like a triple, then he'll shoot off.

BENNY. I'll do it.

BENNY *takes the glass and pours a brandy.*

BERNIE. It's not cold. Just a bit damp.

BENNY. That's summer for you. I'd rather be anywhere than here – Paris, New York, Rome.

BERNIE. You sound like a perfume bottle, Benny.

BENNY *glances at him as he takes the brandy out into the garden.*

It's very kind of you to do this, Guy. Very decent.

GUY. I just thought people might want somewhere to go after the wake. It's nothing.

BERNIE. It's very nice of you, though. Very nice.

GUY. I think I ought to see Daniel –

BERNIE. We don't get much of a chance to chat, do we, Guy?

GUY. Don't we?

BERNIE. Benny's the one people warm to. He's more gregarious than me. One of the lads, and I don't begrudge it. It's a sort of compliment, if you think about it, because I do love him. Could I hold you, Guy?

GUY *is momentarily thrown.*

Just for a second?

GUY. Yes.

> BERNIE *gauchely puts his arms round him.* GUY *can't relax. A moment's awkwardness, then* BERNIE *lets go.*

BERNIE. Thank you for that. I'm scared to death, Guy.

GUY. Why?

BERNIE. I don't want to lose him.

GUY. Why should you? You said everything was fine.

BERNIE; He's always been something of a free spirit, you might say. Amazing we've lasted as long as we have. If I dwell upon what he's got up to, what he might still be getting up to . . . breaks my heart, Guy, it does really. I put up with it, of course, and most of the time, I'm probably imagining it. Do you think I am?

GUY. I'm sure you are.

BERNIE. I could kill him sometimes. Doesn't take me seriously, Guy.

GUY. Of course he does.

BERNIE. Doesn't seem to realise that I have feelings too. I still fancy him, you know, But we haven't done it in a long time. He'll play around once too often. He will really and I'd show him the door, Guy. I would. It's the last thing I want, but I'd do it. Maybe I'm a little naive, but I like to think two people should be sufficient unto themselves, so to speak.

Beat.

GUY. I really ought to go and see Daniel.

BERNIE. I spent a night with Reg.

GUY. What?

BERNIE. I did, Guy. I spent a night with him. The only time I've done such a thing and he's dead!

GUY. When?

BERNIE. Just after your flatwarming. I say a night – forty-five minutes, actually, and I have to admit I'd never felt like that before and doubt I will again, but now I have to ask myself, 'Was it worth it?' and I have to answer, 'No'. It certainly was not, Guy. Once, that's all! Just the once! And I might die because of it.

Enter DANIEL *through the conservatory.*

DANIEL. He's not still in the bog?

GUY. He's in the kitchen. I'll get him. I've got to check the food, anyway.

BERNIE. Need a hand?

GUY. No, I'll be fine.

He exits. Beat.

BERNIE. I'm sure he could do with a spare pair. Better go and see.

He exits. DANIEL *sips his drink. Enter* JOHN.

DANIEL. Where have you been hiding yourself?

JOHN. I haven't.

DANIEL. I've got to go in a minute.

JOHN. How are you?

DANIEL. Marvellous. I've just cremated my lover. What a fucking nightmare!

JOHN. Yeah.

Beat.

DANIEL. Thanks for going to the hospital. I'm sure he appreciated it.

JOHN. Good.

DANIEL. I don't know what I'm going to do. Everything, the smallest thing'll make me miss him. (*He has another sip.*) Do you want a drink?

JOHN. I'll do it.

DANIEL. No, let me. Scotch?

JOHN. Yes. Thanks.

DANIEL *pours a scotch.*

DANIEL. Isn't it incredible? After all these years, the three of us can still be here for each other. It's the best thing in the world. Guy's such a sweetie, isn't he?

JOHN. Yes.

DANIEL. One of the nicest people I know.

He hands JOHN *his drink.*

Cheers!

JOHN. Cheers!

They drink.

DANIEL. I'm off to Spain next week.

JOHN. Whereabouts?

DANIEL. Seville. Some art fair or other. Maybe I'll cancel.

JOHN. It might do you good.

DANIEL. Would you come with me?

Beat.

We could go together. I mean, the art fair business – I can get through that in a matter of hours. And we could have a car – go into the mountains. Or just stay in the city. Whatever.

JOHN. I'm not sure . . .

DANIEL. No. Well.

Beat.

Don't lose touch. Not again.

JOHN. No.

DANIEL. I think he was having an affair.

JOHN. Was he?

DANIEL. The last year or so. Something wasn't right. I should have sorted it out. Too late now. I got it in my head that he was being unfaithful. Not the odd bit on the side – I don't think there was and I never asked because I didn't want to know – but that he was actually having an affair.

JOHN *lights a cigarette.*

And it got to the point where I'd convinced myself he was in love with somebody else. The stupid thing is – and this is what I regret – I couldn't confront him about it, I suppose because I couldn't face it and was hoping he wouldn't do that to me. Then when he was dying and the things he was saying to me, I felt ashamed. He wouldn't have done that to me, would he? You don't think he was having an affair, do you, John?

Pause.

JOHN. I'm sure he wasn't.

DANIEL breaks down. JOHN puts his arms round him.

DANIEL. Even when he was lying there, all skin and bones, looking like his grandfather, I couldn't stop myself thinking about it, staring into those half-dead eyes, wondering if he'd cheated.

JOHN. Daniel . . . Dan . . .

DANIEL. He told me he loved me over and over again. I suppose that's what matters, isn't it?

Beat.

JOHN. Yeah.

DANIEL. Oh, John . . .

Enter BENNY from the garden.

BENNY. It's quite nice out there now . . . sorry.

DANIEL and JOHN disengage as BERNIE enters with an air freshener.

BERNIE. It's quite a spread, I must say! I don't know about you boys, but I could eat a scabby horse, as my Aunty Jean used to say. She was Scottish.

He starts spraying.

BENNY. What the fuck are you doing?

BERNIE. Smells like an ashtray.

BENNY. Smells like a brothel now.

The doorbell rings.

DANIEL. I'm off.

BERNIE. You should eat something, you know. Keep your strength up.

DANIEL. Later, maybe. Thanks.

He kisses BERNIE, *then* BENNY.

Thank you.

BENNY. See you.

DANIEL *kisses* JOHN.

DANIEL. Bye, darling.

JOHN. Bye.

GUY *leads* ERIC *in, who's carrying a bottle of wine.*

BENNY. Hello, Eric.

ERIC. Hello.

DANIEL. I'm off.

He kisses GUY, *as* JOHN *goes into the garden.*

GUY. I'll see you out.

DANIEL. Don't bother. Thank you.

GUY. We'll talk later.

DANIEL. Yeah.

He exits.

BERNIE. Poor Daniel!

ERIC (*handing* GUY *the bottle*). I brought you this. I thought you might need cheering up.

GUY. That's sweet of you. Thanks.

BERNIE. Did you know Reg?

ERIC. No, but Guy mentioned last night he had a funeral on today. Anyway, I'm not stopping.

GUY. Are you working tonight?

ERIC. No.

GUY. Then stay. At least have a drink.

BENNY (*going to the drinks table*). What do you fancy, Eric?

ERIC. Dunno. Coke?

BENNY. Have something stronger! What about a scotch?

BERNIE. Eric's allowed to have a soft drink if he wants, Benny.

ERIC. Alright then. With Coke in.

BENNY (*pouring*). This'll put hair on your chest. Or maybe you don't need it.

ERIC. Someone's parked outside without a permit.

BERNIE. It doesn't apply after six.

GUY. You're not a policeman yet.

BENNY. But when you are, will you promise me something?

ERIC. What?

BENNY. That you'll let me see your helmet.

He hands him the drink.

Bottoms up!

ERIC. Ta.

GUY. Anyway, whoever the culprit is can't be here. No-one's come in their car.

BENNY. Speak for yourself!

BERNIE. Benny! I think you've had enough.

GUY. Food should be about ten minutes.

BERNIE. How's The Frog and Trumpet, Eric?

ERIC. Alright. I haven't seen you in there for ages.

BERNIE. We don't go out as much as we used to.

ERIC. It's still the same.

BERNIE. Becoming quite a permanent fixture there, aren't you?

ERIC. Not for much longer, I hope.

BERNIE. My father wanted to join the force, you know, but he didn't have the feet for it. Took up chiropody instead.

ERIC. Someone was asking after you a few weeks ago.

BERNIE. Really? Who?

ERIC. Posh bloke. Robert something-or-other?

GUY. Ford?

ERIC. That sounds right.

BENNY. Robert Ford?

BERNIE. I don't know him.

ERIC. Maybe it was Benny.

GUY. A few weeks ago?

ERIC. A month or so.

BERNIE. Do I know him, Benny?

BENNY. How the fuck should I know? If you don't know who you know, no-one else fucking will. (*To* ERIC.) He's a lord, you know.

GUY. That's not true. We just called him that because he had a receding chin and a stupid accent.

BENNY. And a fucking prodigious ejaculation! He was in a Chinese restaurant once –

GUY. Benny –

BERNIE. What Chinese restaurant?

BENNY. I don't fucking know. What the fuck do you ask me that for?

BERNIE. Because I haven't heard this before, Benny, that's all. You've never mentioned it.

BENNY. I don't have to tell you everything, do I?

BERNIE. There's no need to be obstreperous.

BENNY. But it's such a stupid fucking question! 'What Chinese restaurant?' What's it fucking matter? The Bridge on the River Kwai in Streatham High Street! Will that do you?

BERNIE. And who is Robert Ford, anyway?

BENNY. If you don't fucking know him, why the fuck do you want to know what Chinese restaurant he was in?

BERNIE. It's been a very distressing day, Benny.

BENNY. I've lost my flow now.

ERIC. Chinese restaurant.

BENNY. What?

ERIC. That's where you'd got to. He was in a Chinese restaurant.

BERNIE. It isn't in China, anyway.

BENNY. What isn't?

BERNIE. The River Kwai.

GUY. Benny –

ERIC. Go on. Tell us.

GUY. He's dead.

Beat.

BENNY. You're kidding!

ERIC. Dead?

BENNY. When?

GUY. Ten days ago.

BENNY. Fuck me!

Beat. BERNIE starts crying.

What's up? You didn't even fucking know him!

BERNIE. How did you know him?

BENNY. What d'you mean?

BERNIE. How did you know him!

BENNY. I met him in the pub.

BERNIE. Is that all?

BENNY. Give it a rest, Bernie!

BERNIE. I want to know!

BENNY. What's it matter? He's fucking dead!

Beat

BERNIE. Goodbye, Guy. Thank you.

BENNY. What you doing?

BERNIE. Eric, see you again, no doubt.

BENNY. Where you off to?

BERNIE. Has it ever crossed your mind that some people might find even me a little bit attractive? One or two have in the past, you know, Benny. And he made me feel a darned sight better than you do most of the time! I really don't want to lose you.

He leaves. Pause. BENNY *replenishes his glass.*

BENNY. Bit of air.

He goes into the garden. Beat. ERIC *wanders over to the conservatory entrance and casts his eye around.*

ERIC. It'll need a fresh coat soon.

GUY. Do you think so?

ERIC. Got a bit flakey at the edges.

GUY. It'll have to wait, I'm afraid.

ERIC. You shouldn't play around, should you?

GUY. What do you mean?

ERIC. If you're with someone, you shouldn't do it. Eric's Norman's playing up.

GUY. Eric's Norman . . . ?

ERIC. Landlord at The Frog. He should never have asked him to move in. I think he's starting to regret it now an' all. I quite like Norman, but he's a bit of a slut.

GUY. Which Norman do you mean? I always get confused.

ERIC. Short hair and no knickers.

GUY. That's the entire clientèle.

ERIC. The other Norman's black.

GUY. Yes, of course.

ERIC. Anyway, Eric's Norman's turned the whole place into a knocking-shop. I don't know how Eric puts up with it cos he must've noticed. I've seen Norman take blokes up to the flat, down to the cellar, into the bogs. I couldn't stand for that, could you?

GUY. I shouldn't think so.

Beat.

ERIC. You ever had a bloke? In a relationship, like?

GUY. No. I haven't.

ERIC. I'm surprised.

GUY. Why?

ERIC. You're nice.

GUY. I could say the same about you.

ERIC. I'm young, though. I've got loads of time. Can I have a top-up?

GUY. Help yourself.

ERIC. What about you?

GUY. I'm fine, thank you.

ERIC *pours a drink.*

ERIC. Have you ever been in love?

GUY. Have you?

ERIC. There was this girl called Janice from Handsworth. I was eight, but we didn't do much about it. Then there was a bloke at school called Dwight, but he'd have smashed my face off as soon as look at me, and since then, well . . .

Beat.

Cheers!

GUY. Cheers!

They drink.

ERIC. So have you?

Beat.

GUY. I met someone . . . oh, nearly fifteen years ago now at university. We've seen each other only a handful of times since then. I don't even know him that well. Yet hardly a

day's passed without me thinking about him. He doesn't feel
the same about me. I know he likes me, but then quite a few
people do. I sometimes think I'd rather be fancied than liked.

ERIC. You wouldn't if you were.

GUY. I'd like the chance to find out.

ERIC. It's John, isn't it?

GUY. Yes.

ERIC. I could tell by the way you are with him.

GUY. That obvious, am I?

ERIC. No. I could just tell.

GUY. The first time I saw him was in a queue in the Refectory.
He was wearing a rugby shirt and jeans and a pair of dirty
plimsolls. He ordered sausages, beans and a double portion of
chips, gooseberry crumble and ice-cream, and a carton of
milk. He was with a couple of mates who were a bit loud,
but there was something about him – the way he picked up
his cutlery, handed over his money, the smile he gave the
cashier . . . I was in such a state, I put custard on my quiche.
And that was it! Not long after, we became friendly through
Daniel, who spotted him in a gay pub. Imagine the hysteria
that caused! You see, John was incredible. He didn't seem to
care. One minute, he'd be playing rugby, the next, he'd be
tonguing a fresher in the Union loo. He got a bit of aggro, but
he could certainly stand up for himself and eventually, people
thought twice. He's always had a reserve; something
untouchable.

Beat.

He's the only one. Can you understand that? Daniel thinks
I'm mad and occasionally I've wondered if I'm imagining it.
But it's stood the test of time and I have to believe it. It
sounds stupid, doesn't it? Do you think it sounds stupid?

ERIC. Have you ever told him?

GUY. No.

ERIC. But you've got to! Just think if you were run down by a
bus tomorrow!

GUY. That's hardly likely. Unless Benny were driving it.

ERIC. Hang on.

He goes into the garden.

GUY. Eric, what are you doing? Eric!

He sips his drink.

Jesus!

He takes another sip. Enter JOHN.

JOHN. Eric said you wanted a word.

GUY. Did he? Are you alright?

JOHN. Yeah.

He lights a cigarette.

He's cute.

GUY. Yes. Yes, he is.

JOHN. So what did you want?

GUY. Nothing really.

JOHN. Up to my eyes in it, aren't I?

Beat.

GUY. If you want a bit of company, if you ever want to stay, you know you're welcome.

JOHN. Yeah. Thanks. Do you know, I've never understood why someone hasn't snapped you up?

GUY. Really?

JOHN. Yes. I mean, you're such a nice guy, you're so . . . It's not fair, is it? Still, it'll happen one day, I'm sure. Do you see much of him?

GUY. Who?

JOHN. Eric.

GUY. From time to time. Mainly at the pub.

JOHN. What about him?

GUY. What do you mean?

JOHN. Have you ever thought about giving Eric a go?

GUY. As you say, he's . . . cute, but –

JOHN. He can only say no and he likes you, doesn't he?

GUY. I think so, but 'like' isn't the issue.

Beat.

The way some of these young ones look at me, or not, as the
case may be! I know I'm nearly forty, but my dick hasn't
dropped off.

Beat.

But yes, he's cute. You're right.

JOHN. You should tell him.

GUY. Yes, maybe I should.

JOHN. Anyway, you deserve someone.

GUY. John?

JOHN. Yes?

Beat.

GUY. You remember 'The Bacchae'?

JOHN. Mm?

GUY. And the last night party, when we were up in the flies?

JOHN. Up in the flies . . . Yes! I remember! That little scumbag
playing . . . whatever it was –

GUY. Pentheus.

JOHN. That's it! He chucked his ring, didn't he?

GUY. Yes, but I meant before that.

JOHN. Before he threw up?

GUY. Before he arrived.

JOHN. Right.

Beat.

GUY. We were having a bit of a chat.

JOHN. Uh-huh.

GUY. We were . . . well, you said something –

JOHN. Do you know, some bastard nicked my jockstrap?

GUY. Did they?

JOHN. Yeah! Not that I wanted it, but . . . sorry, what were you saying?

GUY. Up in the flies, we were having a chat and a bottle of wine and you were telling me about yourself.

JOHN. What did I say?

GUY. Lots of things.

JOHN. Was I pissed?

GUY. Not particularly. And after a while, you said something to me that I thought meant that you might want to . . .

JOHN. What?

GUY. That I thought meant you might . . .

Beat.

Do you remember?

JOHN. I remember Pentheus throwing up.

Beat.

GUY. He was a bit of a pain, wasn't he?

JOHN. Yeah.

Beat.

He's left me nothing, you know.

Beat.

GUY. Well, it'd have been a bit difficult, wouldn't it? Daniel not knowing and everything.

JOHN. But I can't help wondering. I haven't loved anyone before. He knocked me for six. The first time in my life when I felt I wasn't in control. Do you think he loved me?

GUY. I wouldn't know. I hardly ever saw you together and he never talked about it because he didn't know I knew.

JOHN. Did you like him?

GUY. Yes.

JOHN. Really?

GUY. Yes. Well, I suppose my opinion of him went down a bit after you'd told me about the two of you.

JOHN. Did your opinion of me go down a bit?

GUY. No.

JOHN. Why not? We were both shitting on Daniel.

Beat.

GUY. To be honest, I did think you should've told him, but you're going to, aren't you?

JOHN. It's over now. Why disillusion him?

GUY. But in one sense, it's not over, is it? Dan'll carry on talking about him and we'll carry on lying.

JOHN. That's better than spoiling it for him. He was happy with Reg. So was I. Why fuck it up?

GUY. Maybe this isn't the best time to talk about it. You've had the most awful day –

JOHN. And if I do tell him – and I'm not saying I never will – how much should I tell him? All of it? Part of it? Once I'd started, where would I stop?

GUY. But I can't help feeling that Reg was having his cake and eating it.

JOHN. What's it matter?

GUY. Quite a few cakes, by all accounts.

Beat.

JOHN. What?

GUY. Well . . . he wasn't exactly a saint, was he?

JOHN. What do you mean?

GUY. I'm not telling you anything new.

JOHN. What are you telling me?

GUY. Nothing.

JOHN. Guy!

GUY. I suppose all I'm saying is that if he could do that to Daniel, why couldn't he do it to you?

JOHN. He was having an affair?

GUY. No, no! I'm just telling you what you already know.

JOHN. And what's that?

GUY. That fidelity wasn't exactly his strong point.

JOHN. Wasn't it?

GUY. For Christ's sake, John, the very fact that he had an affair with you!

JOHN. Who else?

GUY. I don't know.

JOHN. Who?

GUY. No-one!

JOHN pours a scotch.

I'm sorry. It's not my place . . .

He gulps it down.

I just didn't like the way he treated you – both of you. That's all.

JOHN pours another.

You just can't carry on like that.

He gulps it down.

This is the wrong time. We really shouldn't be talking about it.

JOHN. Even if he did . . . a bit on the side . . . what's it matter? It doesn't take anything away . . . What the fuck's it matter?

GUY. But it does matter! What the hell was he playing at? It was so irresponsible. Even the vicar told me what a good fuck he was outside the crematorium! God, I'm sorry. I'm sorry. I didn't mean to say that. I'm sorry. It's because I'm worried about you, about Daniel and the lot of you. I'm sorry. I really didn't mean to.

JOHN. One minute! I mean, what do you say to someone when you know it's the last time?

GUY. John –

JOHN. What do you say? I leant over, smelt his hair, kissed his
cheek, managed to say, 'I love you' and before he could say
anything, Daniel had come back. He told me hundreds of
times he loved me, but the one time that would've mattered
was the last and Daniel came back to the bedside. Maybe he
didn't in the end. When you're dying, maybe things fall into
place and Dan was the only person who counted –

GUY. John –

JOHN. And now I'll never know.

Beat.

You're probably thinking, 'I could have told you so'. But
those few years – it could've been a night and it'd have been
worth it.

Beat.

I'm frightened.

GUY. Yes.

Beat. He touches JOHN's *arm.* JOHN *doesn't respond.*
BENNY *and* ERIC *come back in.* GUY *starts sniffing.*

Oh God! I'm sorry. Something's burning. (*Extricating
himself from the embrace.*) Sorry.

He dashes out. The rain starts again. BENNY *goes to* JOHN.

BENNY. Do you want a drink?

JOHN *shakes his head.* BENNY *puts an arm around him.*

Fucking summer!

ERIC *goes to the door.*

ERIC. Do you want any help?

GUY (*off*). No. No, thanks.

ERIC *glances at* JOHN *and* BENNY. *He's not sure what to
do. Then he looks through* GUY's *records.*

BENNY. Can I bum a fag?

JOHN *offers him one.* BENNY *takes two and puts them in his
mouth.* JOHN *lights them, then* BENNY *puts one in* JOHN's
mouth, keeping the other for himself.

I owe you 'undreds.

BENNY *saunters over to the conservatory entrance.*

I kinda see what Bernie's talking about. Nice, isn't it?

JOHN *goes over and stands next to him.*

Like your own fuckin' jungle.

JOHN*'s crying quietly.*

Oh dear. Got you bad, hasn't it?

He puts his arms round JOHN. JOHN *puts his round* BENNY, *still crying.*

There you go. That's right.

ERIC *looks at them, then returns to the records.* BENNY *strokes* JOHN*'s hair.* JOHN*'s crying begins to subside.*

That's right.

BENNY *rubs his face against* JOHN*'s hair. He gently kisses it.* JOHN *raises his face and brushes it against* BENNY*'s.*

Yeah. That's right.

BENNY *takes a drag on his cigarette and throws it into the conservatory. He gently takes* JOHN*'s cigarette off him, drags on it, then throws that into the conservatory. He kisses* JOHN*'s face several times, ending up at his mouth. They kiss gently on the lips, then passionately.* ERIC *watches them, then goes to the drinks table and pours himself a stiff one.* GUY *enters, distressed.*

GUY. A complete fucking incineration! It'll have to be a take-away.

He clocks BENNY *and* JOHN. BENNY *gently ends the kiss and, still in the embrace, looks at* GUY.

BENNY. He's alright. Don't worry. He'll be fine.

His arm round JOHN, *he leads him into the conservatory.* GUY *watches them.*

ERIC. Can I get you something?

GUY. No. Gin. Thank you.

ERIC *obliges.*

I can't believe it. The timer didn't go off. Cost me a fortune. It hasn't quite worked out as planned. I can't believe it. You can't trust anyone. They only installed it last week.

He looks towards the conservatory.

Are you hungry? The salad and cheese are still intact. Would you like some?

ERIC (*handing him his drink*). I'm fine, thanks.

GUY. Are you sure?

ERIC. I picked up a burger on the way.

GUY. Just as well. Cheers!

ERIC. Cheers!

They sip their drinks. GUY glances again at the conservatory.

Nice records.

GUY. Oh. Yes.

ERIC. I haven't heard of most of them.

GUY. Play one if you like.

ERIC. Did you tell him?

GUY. What?

ERIC. What you were going to?

GUY. No. Not exactly.

He sits on the sofa.

Fuck it, I'm nearly forty! What if I reach fifty and still haven't met anyone? I'm nothing to write home about now – God knows what I'll be like then. Dogs'll probably bark at me in the street.

ERIC. You're not that bad.

He glances into the conservatory.

Funny, isn't it? Just when you think you've got a handle on things, it all pisses off in another direction.

GUY. What?

ERIC. I'm a bit rat-arsed.

He sits next to GUY.

GUY. Are you?

ERIC. When you work in a pub, people think you drink all the time, but you don't. Except for Norman. He's always shoving one up the Optics. But I'm not used to it. I stick to Coke. Haven't had this much in ages.

He rests his head back and closes his eyes. GUY looks at him, then towards the conservatory, then back at ERIC. The rain is still pouring down onto the conservatory roof. GUY tentatively moves a hand towards ERIC's knee.

(*His eyes still shut.*) D'you know something?

GUY instantly withdraws his hand, having not made contact.

GUY. What?

ERIC. I like you.

GUY. Do you?

ERIC. You're not like the others, thinking about sex all the time. I mean, how can you judge a bloke by the shape of his bum or the size of his packet?

GUY. You can't.

Beat.

Well, maybe not the whole person.

He looks back to the conservatory.

I hope they're not killing my plants.

He looks back at ERIC whose eyes are still closed. His gaze works slowly down his whole body.

ERIC. I was a choirboy.

GUY. Were you?

ERIC. I did solos. The organist was very encouraging. Gave me the odd private lesson.

GUY. Really?

ERIC. He had incredible hands. Small, but versatile. Comes with the job, I suppose. You can't just die, though, can you? There must be something else.

GUY. Do you think so?

ERIC. Wouldn't make sense, otherwise. Like, while we're pissing around, getting our knickers in a twist, it's all going on anyway, isn't it? Whatever we do.

Beat.

Like, it's night now, then it'll be morning.

Beat.

I'm pissed.

GUY. Can I kiss you? I'm sorry, I didn't mean that. Can I? I shouldn't have said that. I'm sorry.

He puts his hand on ERIC's *knee, then withdraws it.*

Sorry.

He looks towards the conservatory. ERIC *looks at him. Beat. Then* GUY *looks at* ERIC.

ERIC. It's like me mum asking for a snog.

Beat.

I didn't mean that nastily. Just a bit surprised. I've never thought of you like that. I don't think I can.

Beat.

Mum's dead, actually.

Beat.

Sorry.

Beat.

GUY. Would you stay the night? Not to do anything. Just lie together. Would you do that?

Beat.

ERIC. You mean, just sleeping in the same bed?

GUY. Yes. Would you?

Beat.

ERIC. Yeah.

GUY. Good. Thanks.

He looks at the conservatory, then back at ERIC.

Can I get you anything?

ERIC. I spent a night with someone once. Year or so ago. It was the first time I really did it. Properly, you know. It was very nice. I thought, I've saved myself up for this and I've made the right decision. What he said to me, what he did to me, even though it was only the first time we'd met, I thought, this is the one. But he never saw me again and I got the impression he wasn't telling me the whole story. Some people don't have any scruples, do they?

GUY. What was his name?

ERIC. He said names didn't matter, I could call him anything I wanted. So I called him Dwight, after that boy at school. The only other name I could think of was Janice, but that'd have been a bit daft.

Enter BENNY *and* JOHN *from the conservatory.*

JOHN. We're off.

GUY. Right. I could rustle something up. You haven't eaten anything.

BENNY. I'm not hungry.

GUY. The timer went all to fuck.

JOHN. Thanks, Guy.

He embraces him, then:

GUY. Bye, Benny.

GUY *kisses* BENNY.

BENNY. Thanks a lot. Tara, Eric.

ERIC. Bye.

JOHN. Bye.

They've gone. Beat.

GUY. How about a cup of tea?

The phone rings. GUY *answers it.*

Hello? . . . (*Quietly.*) Oh . . . Yeah . . . Look, Brad, I'm a bit tied up . . . Tomorrow . . . Brad, it's not . . . (*Very quietly.*) Down, boy! . . . Okay? . . . Bye.

He replaces the receiver.

Tea?

ERIC. Ta.

GUY *exits.* ERIC *goes to the records and looks through them again. He picks one out. He takes it out of the sleeve and puts it on the turntable. He puts the stylus on the record. The second movement of Ravel's Piano Concerto in G Major starts playing.* GUY *enters almost immediately.*

GUY. Why have you put that on?

ERIC. It was Dwight's favourite. He played it to me when the sun was coming up. He said it'd always remind him of me.

Beat.

It'd be nice to see him again, even from a distance.

Beat.

Wonder what he's up to?

The music continues as the rain keeps falling and the lights fade.

Scene Three

The music continues. Dawn. The rain has reduced to a drizzle pattering onto the roof of the conservatory. ERIC leans against the conservatory entrance, naked, looking out at the garden and listening to the music. At one point, he slowly, elegantly raises his arm as if executing a dance movement. Then he continues listening. JOHN appears at the doorway, naked and dishevelled, just roused from sleep. ERIC doesn't notice him. He seems disturbed. He glances round the room, then focuses on the record-player. He takes the record off. ERIC looks round.

ERIC. What did you do that for?

JOHN. Why are you playing this?

ERIC. It's nice.

Beat.

Are you alright?

JOHN. I was dreaming, then heard that. I got a bit confused.

Beat.

What time is it?

ERIC. Dunno. About five, I think.

JOHN. Why are you up?

ERIC shrugs. JOHN retrieves a dressing-gown from a pile of clothes and puts it on.

You'll catch cold.

ERIC. It's summer..

Beat.

JOHN. I'm sorry I wasn't . . . The booze and everything . . .

ERIC. I was pissed an' all.

JOHN. Yeah.

ERIC. I didn't want to anyway.

JOHN. Didn't you?

ERIC. No.

JOHN. Why not?

ERIC. I'd have felt guilty, wouldn't I? Cup of tea?

JOHN. Yes.

> ERIC *goes out.* JOHN *searches for a cigarette. He looks through a few empty packets before finding one. He lights it, inhales, coughs, grimaces, then inhales again. He takes a pile of photographs from a drawer and slowly looks through them.* ERIC *returns.*

ERIC. Done in a tick.

> *Beat.* ERIC *looks through the pile of clothes, finds a pair of underpants and puts them on.*

Can I have a fag?

JOHN (*pointing to the packet.*) There's some in there.

> ERIC *takes one.*

ERIC. Got a light?

JOHN (*giving him a light*). I didn't think you smoked.

ERIC. I don't, but everyone I know who doesn't's dead. What are those?

JOHN. A few photos of university. I came across them a day or two ago.

ERIC. Let's have a look.

> JOHN *gives them to him.*

JOHN (*pointing to a photo*). There's Dan, Guy, and there's me.

ERIC. Had people used to look like that?

JOHN. What does that mean?

ERIC. Isn't Guy's hair long? Ugh! Daniel's wearing flares! Don't he look horrible! Is that you?

JOHN. Yes.

ERIC. God, you look young!

JOHN *takes them off him.*

I was enjoying them.

Beat.

I wonder if I'd've enjoyed university. No-one ever went from our school. I got four CSEs, mind you. Did you enjoy it?

JOHN. Yes, I did.

ERIC. Which school did you go to?

JOHN. Marlborough.

ERIC. Is that a public school?

JOHN. Yeah.

ERIC. I guessed as much.

JOHN. Why?

ERIC. You're that sort, aren't you?

JOHN. Am I?

ERIC. I don't mean it nastily. Did you see 'Another Country'?

JOHN. Yes.

ERIC. I loved that film. All them posh blokes bonking. Was it like that at your school?

JOHN. A little bit.

ERIC. You didn't get it at Erdington Comprehensive. If they thought you were a pouf, they chucked you in the canal and pissed on you.

JOHN. Did they do that to you?

ERIC. No. They never found out. I got thrown out of a window.

JOHN. Why?

ERIC. I think they were a bit bored.

JOHN. Did you get hurt?

ERIC. No. It was only the first floor. I'll get the tea.

He goes out. JOHN *glances at a few more photos, puts them aside and sits down.* ERIC *returns with two mugs of tea and gives one to* JOHN.

JOHN. Thanks.

ERIC sits next to him. They sip their tea.

ERIC. Everyone was arseholed, weren't they?

JOHN. Yes.

ERIC. Bernie was on another planet! He's like this woman
I knew when I was a kid. She hung around outside the
playground singing at the top of her voice – opera and stuff –
and she always had a bunch of lilies. If you got too close, she
hit you on the head with them.

JOHN. I don't think Bernie's got to that point.

ERIC. Well, he's not singing yet, but I didn't know where to put
myself when he ran up to the coffin and chucked a lily on it.
Just when it was going through the doors an' all! I thought he
was going through with it for a minute. Benny should never
have brought Conrad. I mean, he didn't even know Guy and
he must've realised that Bernie was going to take the hump. I
hate that Conrad. Can't understand what Benny sees in him.

Beat.

Benny's changed, hasn't he? He's like a little wife. Just what
Bernie always wanted him to be. He should never have kicked
him out. Doesn't know what to do with himself now. Lonely
as fuck and miserable as sin! I found him in the garden at one
point chatting up the oleander. Then he told me he was
thinking of joining the Salvation Army. I reckon he's two
bricks short of a load.

Beat.

He was so fond of Guy! He came in the pub after he'd heard
Guy'd been taken ill. He was in such a state, Eric and I had to
take him upstairs.

Beat.

Can't believe it, can you? It just doesn't make sense. I mean,
it's not as if he put it around a lot. He didn't seem to, anyway.
Mind you, I suppose I didn't know him that well.

JOHN. Neither did I.

ERIC looks at him.

You're right. He didn't put it around. He was extremely careful. In fact, when I went to see him in hospital, he put it down to an encounter he had on holiday . . . oh, years ago now. Not that it matters. But I guess you can't help thinking about it.

Beat.

ERIC. Nice flowers.

JOHN. Yes.

ERIC. Did you see that bouquet in the shape of a bone? I wonder who sent that.

JOHN. He was there, actually. Brad. The one in the leather collar.

ERIC. I thought he was a vicar.

JOHN. Nobody knows what he is. Even Guy didn't; they never met.

ERIC. You won't tell Eric, will you?

JOHN. What?

ERIC. That I stayed the night.

JOHN. That's all you have done.

ERIC. He had his fingers burnt with Norman, I can tell you! Best thing he did giving him the elbow. You mustn't say anything. You won't, will you?

JOHN. Of course I won't.

ERIC. I don't want him getting suspicious.

JOHN. When's he back?

ERIC. When his mother gets out of traction. We're making a go of it, see, and I think it's working out alright. I've got quite accustomed to the idea of running a pub since the police turned me down. I've had a few ideas an' all.

JOHN. I've thought about getting a pub . . . or a restaurant or something.

ERIC. So why don't you?

JOHN. Maybe I will.

ERIC (*looking at him*). You're odd, you are.

JOHN. Am I?

ERIC. Keep yourself to yourself, don't you?

No response.

Do you ever open up?

JOHN. Sometimes.

Beat.

ERIC. You and Guy never sort of . . .

JOHN. What?

ERIC. Had a thing together, did you?

JOHN. No.

ERIC. It's amazing, isn't it? Leaving you his flat and everything.

Beat.

He loved you, you know. He said you were the only one.

Beat.

JOHN. I've found piles of photographs of me; discarded
notebooks from university that he must have taken from
my room; write-ups of matches that I played; a bottle of
aftershave – I still remember missing that; a comb; a shirt; an
old biro that I used during Finals with my teethmarks on it;
even a leather jockstrap I wore in a play. I found all this stuff
in a case on top of the wardrobe. It was the weirdest thing.

ERIC. He'd have only done it cos of what he felt for you. And
you felt nothing for him?

JOHN. Of course I did. He was a mate. The nicest man.

ERIC. But you didn't love him or anything?

JOHN. He should've said something.

ERIC. What would you have done?

JOHN. I don't know.

Beat.

ERIC. Have you ever been in love?

JOHN. Yeah.

ERIC. Who with?

JOHN. Nosey little fucker, aren't you?

ERIC. Sorry.

> JOHN *holds his hand.*

JOHN. A man called Reg.

ERIC. Reg?

JOHN. Yes.

> *Beat.*

ERIC. You mean . . . ?

JOHN. Yes.

> *Beat.*

ERIC. Oh.

> JOHN *lifts* ERIC's *hand to his lips and kisses it.*

> When?

JOHN. The last few years of his life.

ERIC. And did you actually . . . do it, like?

JOHN. All the time.

ERIC. Oh.

> *He licks* ERIC's *fingers.*

> Did Daniel know?

JOHN. Not a clue.

ERIC. Did anyone?

JOHN. Guy. He was the only one.

ERIC. Oh.

> JOHN *touches* ERIC's *knee.*

> John . . .

JOHN. What?

He slides his hand up ERIC'*s thigh.*

ERIC. Will you ever tell him?

JOHN. You think I should?

ERIC. Yeah.

JOHN. So did Guy. So do I.

ERIC. So will you?

JOHN'*s hand reaches* ERIC'*s crotch.* ERIC *pushes it away.*

JOHN. I've never faced up to responsibilities.

ERIC. You've got to sometime though, haven't you?

Beat.

You must tell him. It's only fair. You're friends, for Christ's sake! You'd feel better for it, as well.

JOHN. You're right.

He puts his arm round ERIC'*s shoulder.* ERIC *resists.*

Please . . .

Beat. ERIC *stops resisting. Then* JOHN *gently draws* ERIC'*s head onto his shoulder.* ERIC *resists again.*

ERIC. No.

JOHN. It's alright. We're not doing anything.

Beat. ERIC *tentatively submits, letting his head rest on* JOHN'*s shoulder.* JOHN *strokes his hair.*

That's alright, isn't it?

Beat.

ERIC. I've been thinking.

JOHN. Have you?

ERIC. The security at The Frog and Trumpet's rubbish.

JOHN. Is it?

ERIC. Cameras. It's the only way. A kiddie could get in there at the moment. I'll have a word with Eric.

JOHN runs his hand down ERIC'*s back.* ERIC *tenses, then relaxes.*

I've also had a thought or two about how to boost business. Cabaret: that's the thing. What do you think?

JOHN. Could be.

ERIC. I haven't told Eric yet, but I'm sure he'll go along with it. I might give it a go myself an' all. Once or twice, y'know; we'd get other acts in too. I've been giving it a lot of thought.

JOHN gently fingers the top of ERIC'*s underpants.*

That music I was listening to, what you turned off, I thought I could start with that and come on as a nymph or something, like they thought it was going to be ballet –

JOHN. I can't quite see you as a nymph.

ERIC. Why not?

JOHN. You're more of a satyr . . .

ERIC. A what?

JOHN. Or a fox . . .

He lets his hand run over ERIC'*s backside.*

Or a dog.

Beat.

ERIC. I'll stick with nymph. Any road, just when everyone was getting a bit bored, the music'd change into Annie Lennox or Dorothy Squires and I'd whip off whatever I had on and there'd be something else underneath and I'd go into this big number. What d'you think?

JOHN eases down ERIC'*s pants.*

John . . .

JOHN. Please . . .

ERIC. I mustn't . . .

JOHN (*stroking* ERIC'*s arse*). Your skin . . . so young . . .

ERIC. Eh?

JOHN. I used to have a bum like yours.

ERIC. You've got a nice bum. Considering.

JOHN. Considering what?

ERIC. Well, you know . . . If I reach your age, I wouldn't mind looking like you.

JOHN. I'm old enough to be your fucking dad!

ERIC. At least you're still here to moan about it!

> JOHN *freezes.*

I'm sorry. I didn't mean . . .

JOHN. Why's he done this? The flat . . . I don't need it. I don't even want it!

ERIC. He loved you.

JOHN. But I didn't love him. I can't help that, can I?

> *Beat.*

I only visited him a couple of times. Couldn't face it . . .

> *Beat.*

The last time I saw him . . . lying on his side, shrivelled up like a little old man . . . he made me lean right down to put my ear against his mouth and he said, 'I love you. I always have,' and I'd never realised before. I must be stupid.

ERIC. No you're not. You can't help not loving him back.

JOHN. That's right, isn't it? I can't help that.

ERIC (*tearful*). We're all going to miss him.

JOHN. The worst thing, Eric . . . the worst thing of all is that when Guy said he loved me that last time I saw him, all I could think was that I wish it'd been Reg.

> *The doorbell rings. They jump.*

ERIC. Fuck me!

JOHN. Who the hell's that?

> JOHN *goes out.* ERIC *rummages through the clothes. The front door's opened.*

DANIEL (*off*). Darling!

JOHN (*off*). Daniel!

DANIEL (*off*). I'd kill for coffee.

Enter DANIEL *and* JOHN *before* ERIC*'s found any clothing.*

(*Clocking* ERIC.) Sweet! Mm! I sniff tumescence.

JOHN. It's five-thirty!

DANIEL. I knew you wouldn't mind.

JOHN. You only left three hours ago.

DANIEL. I couldn't face going home, so I popped up the Heath.

JOHN. It's raining.

DANIEL. Didn't stop anyone. When I left twenty minutes ago, it was still like Nero's Rome. What is it about summer? Plays havoc with the hormones.

JOHN. You're still in your funeral gear.

DANIEL. I could've been in a body-bag and I'd have got laid.

ERIC. I'll make some coffee, shall I?

JOHN. Yes.

DANIEL. That would be divine.

ERIC goes out.

It doesn't look like you two have been discussing Jane Austen.

JOHN. It's not quite as it might seem.

DANIEL. Pretty damned near, I'd say. (*Re.* JOHN*'s dressing-gown.*) Isn't that Guy's?

JOHN. Is it?

Beat.

DANIEL. You managed to get rid of Bernie, then.

JOHN. We shoved him in a taxi just after you'd left.

DANIEL. Poor old queen! Boring as fuck, but you can't help feeling for him. Oh Juanita, what are we to do? Guy of all people! Jesus fucking Christ! Give us a fag.

JOHN. You don't smoke.

DANIEL. What the fuck!

DANIEL starts looking through the records as JOHN finds a cigarette. He lights it and hands it to DANIEL.

Thanks, pet. I tell you, the Heath was so muddy, it was like an icerink. I was doing Sonja Henie impersonations all over the shop. And I lost a lens! I walked into at least half-a-dozen trees. Tried to go down on one of them. But you know how you get – sort of cock crazy. It was like Harrods' sale. You've no idea! Well, maybe more British Home Stores, but who cares? There were plenty of bargains in plenty of basements. And beautiful! Even though it was pissing down. I was moved to do a snatch of Titania at one point until an overweight biker insisted on chewing my nipples off. There was even an encampment of the homeless sitting round a pile of sodden twigs. It was like Act Three of 'Carmen'. (*Taking out a record.*) This is the one.

He puts it on the turntable.

Breakfast disco!

He puts the stylus on the record: 'Starman' by David Bowie. JOHN laughs. DANIEL takes hold of him and they start dancing. DANIEL sings along with it. Eventually, JOHN does too. Then they quieten down, stop dancing and split up. JOHN wanders over to the conservatory and looks out. DANIEL notices the pile of photographs and sombrely looks through them. Then he puts them down and takes off the record before the song's finished. Pause.

So what will you do?

JOHN. I haven't begun to think.

DANIEL. It's mad. The best laid plans etcetera. Mind you, you've never made any.

JOHN. What about you? Will you stay on at the flat?

DANIEL. No. I've stuck it for two years, but whatever I do, I can't get rid of him. Not that I want to in one sense, but trivial reminders are somehow the most melancholic and I don't want to be sad. Why should I be? We had a great time together.

Beat.

This place, though. You could keep it. After all, it doesn't hold any memories particularly and you want to sell Holland Park, so why not?

JOHN. As I say, I haven't given it a thought yet.

DANIEL. What a wonderful thing to do! You know he was mad about you?

JOHN. Why didn't you tell me?

DANIEL. I don't think I believed it and you'd have run a mile.

JOHN. I wouldn't have.

DANIEL. John!

JOHN. We could've talked about it, sorted it out somehow. I don't know –

DANIEL. Did you know Bernie had slept with Reg?

Beat.

JOHN. No.

DANIEL. He told me last night when he was drunk. Bernie of all people! It was the last thing I needed to hear. It's opened up a whole fucking can of worms, I tell you!

Beat.

John?

JOHN. What?

DANIEL. There's something I've been meaning to ask you.

JOHN. Yeah?

DANIEL. Yes. You remember Guy's flatwarming?

JOHN. Yeah.

DANIEL. And you said that you'd bumped into Reg the night before at that film?

Beat.

JOHN. Yeah?

DANIEL. I've always wondered . . . I shouldn't say this . . . oh, fuck it! . . . Well, it seemed such a coincidence and I've always wondered whether you spent the night together. Did

you? It wouldn't matter if you had . . . well, it would, but . . .
I've always been curious. Shit, I don't know what I'm going
on about! I mean, what's a night between friends? But did
you? Did you spend that night with Reg?

Beat.

JOHN. A night with Reg?

DANIEL. Mm.

JOHN. The night before the flatwarming?

DANIEL. Yes.

JOHN. That was ages ago.

DANIEL. That's not the point. You'd still remember.

JOHN. No – I mean, why would you ask that now?

DANIEL. You did, didn't you?

JOHN. Daniel –

DANIEL. Didn't you?

Pause.

JOHN. No. Of course I didn't.

Pause. He tentatively embraces DANIEL. *After a while,*
DANIEL *succumbs to the embrace.*

DANIEL. I'm sorry . . .

JOHN. No, no . . .

DANIEL. Oh . . .

By now, the drizzle's stopped. A bird starts singing.

I'm losing the people I can talk to.

JOHN. You can talk to me.

DANIEL. We've got to keep in touch.

JOHN. Yes.

DANIEL. No – this time, we've got to. I needed you when Guy
was ill. I nearly didn't find you in time. So we will, won't we?

JOHN. Yes, we will.

Beat. They kiss affectionately, then break the embrace.

DANIEL. I think I'll go. I'm suddenly very tired. Apologise to Eric, will you?

JOHN. Yes.

DANIEL *goes to the door.*

Dan?

DANIEL *stops and turns. They look at each other. A couple of other birds have joined in the singing.*

DANIEL. Yes?

Beat.

JOHN. I'm pretty tired, too. I haven't been sleeping too well lately.

Beat.

DANIEL. We'll speak later.

He goes out. The birdsong continues. JOHN *lights a cigarette. Enter* ERIC *with a tray of coffee.*

ERIC. Has he gone?

JOHN. He said sorry. He was a bit knackered.

ERIC *looks at him.* JOHN *looks away.* ERIC *puts the tray down.*

ERIC. How would you like it?

JOHN. Black. Thanks.

ERIC *pours a cup and gives it to* JOHN. *Then he pours himself a cup. He looks again at* JOHN, *who's concentrating on his coffee. The birdsong continues.*

ERIC. Noisy little buggers, aren't they?

No response. ERIC *sips his coffee.*

Want to watch telly?

No response. ERIC *searches out a TV magazine and looks through it.*

There's a pop show, game show, film . . .

JOHN. Which one?

ERIC. Some French thing . . . No . . . Sounds dead boring.

He puts it aside and looks at JOHN *yet again, who still doesn't return the look. Then he goes to the conservatory entrance and looks out.*

It might be sunny today. You could come round the pub for lunch. Sit outside.

JOHN. Yes, I might.

ERIC (*casting his eye over the conservatory*). This needs doing. The garden's a mess an' all. You've got to have them done. Guy'd be furious otherwise.

He looks across at JOHN. *Eventually,* JOHN *looks at him. The birds continue singing. The lights fade.*

End.

A Nick Hern Book

This special programme edition of *My Night with Reg* first
published in Great Britain 1994 by Nick Hern Books Limited,
14 Larden Road, London W3 7ST in association with the Royal
Court Theatre, Sloane Square, London SW1W 8AS

Front cover illustration: photograph copyright Matthew Ward

Typeset by Country Setting. Woodchurch, Kent TN26 3TB
Printed by Cox and Wyman Ltd, Reading, Berks

A CIP catalogue record for this book is available from
the British Library

ISBS 1-85459-272-6

For a complete list of plays and theatre books published
by Nick Hern, please write to Nick Hern Books Limited,
14 Larden Road, London W3 7ST.